From the foreword:

The End of Suffering, by Russell Targ and J. J. Hurtak, is vital for all readers at this time. The authors perform here a great service to humanity by making Nagarjuna's teaching on the end of suffering transparent and accessible to the general reader. They make his profound innovations available and relevant to our lives in today's world. And readers who enter this work will find powerful tools and insights that will empower them to get right to the source of their existential suffering. This important book fills a void and builds a bridge that helps make Buddha's global teachings and Nagarjuna's spiritual technology on the end of suffering a living reality for all who truly wish to help end individual and collective suffering in our human condition.

—Prof. Ashok Gangadean, Philosophy Department, Haverford College

Other Books Authored or Coauthored by Russell Targ

Limitless Mind: A Guide to Remote Viewing and Transformation of Consciousness (2004)

The Heart of the Mind: How to Experience God without Belief (1999, with Jane Katra)

Miracles of Mind: Exploring Nonlocal Consciousness and Spiritual Healing (1998, with Jane Katra)

The Mind Race: Understanding and Using Psychic Abilities (1984, with Keith Harary)

Mind at Large: IEEE Symposia on the Nature of Extrasensory Perception (1979, 2002, with Charles Tart and Harold Puthoff)

Mind-Reach: Scientists Look at Psychic Abilities (1977, 2005, with Harold Puthoff)

Other Books by J. J. Hurtak

Consciousness, Energy, and Future Science (2002, editor)

Pistis Sophia: A Coptic Gnostic Text with Commentary (1999, with Desiree Hurtak)

The Scrolls of Adam & Eve: A Study of Prophetic Regenesis (1989)

The Old Testament Scrolls of Obadiah, Jonah, & Micah: A Study of Prophetic Regenesis (1984)

The Book of Knowledge: The Keys of Enoch® (1973)

Gnosticism: Mystery of Mysteries (1970)

The End of Suffering

Fearless Living in Troubled Times

. . . or, How to Get Out of Hell Free

Russell Targ and J. J. Hurtak, Ph.D.

HAMPTON ROADS
PUBLISHING COMPANY, INC.

Cover concept by Marsha Simms Haisch
Cover painting by Ingo Swann. All rights reserved.

Hampton Roads Publishing Company, Inc.
1125 Stoney Ridge Road
Charlottesville, VA 22902

434-296-2772
fax: 434-296-5096
e-mail: hrpc@hrpub.com
www.hrpub.com

If you are unable to order this book from your local
bookseller, you may order directly from the publisher.
Call 1-800-766-8009, toll-free.

Library of Congress Cataloging-in-Publication Data

Targ, Russell.
The end of suffering : fearless living in troubled times / Russell Targ
and J.J. Hurtak.
    p. cm.
Summary: "Targ and Hurtak examine modern culture's battle of opposites: good or
evil, right or wrong, Democrat or Republican. In an effort to overcome the perceived
polarity of opposites and the accompanying suffering, the authors combine the
wisdom of the East with the finding of quantum physics, uncovering a middle
ground that shows opposing sides are really the same"--Provided by publisher.
Includes bibliographical references and index.
ISBN 1-57174-468-1 (tp : alk. paper)
1. Suffering. 2. Quantum theory. I. Hurtak, J. J. II. Title.
B105.S75T37 2006
128'.4--dc22
                          2005029816

ISBN 1-57174-468-1
10 9 8 7 6 5 4 3
Printed on acid-free paper in the United States

For Patricia and Desiree,
with admiration, appreciation,
and much love

Contents

Cast of Characters and Their Concepts, in Order of Appearance

Aristotle: Greek philosopher who enshrined duality and the law of the "excluded middle."

Duality: The idea that I am who I am, and entirely separate from you: two ideas in opposition.

Nagarjuna: Indian philosopher who showed that most ideas are neither true nor not true.

Nonduality: The nonconceptual view that there is only one of us here in consciousness.

Four-Logic: My truth together with your truth, where the middle is not excluded.

Madhyamika: Middle Path of Buddhism emphasizing compassion and surrender to emptiness.

Einstein: Physicist who perfected relativity but felt uncomfortable with quantum mechanics requiring "a ghostly action at a distance."

Locality: Physical theory that distant objects cannot have direct influence on one another.

J. S. Bell: Physicist who proved that nonlocality could be tested for in the laboratory.

Nonlocality: Universal property by which apparently separate items are still entangled.

We have tried everything to get rid of suffering. We have gone everywhere to get rid of suffering. We have bought everything to get rid of it. We have ingested everything to get rid of it.

Finally, when one has tried enough, there arises the possibility of spiritual maturity with the willingness to stop the futile attempt to get rid of and, instead, to actually experience suffering. In that momentous instant, there is the realization of that which is beyond suffering, of that which is untouched by suffering. There is the realization of who one truly is.

—Gangaji

Foreword:
Nagarjuna and the
End of Global Suffering

Buddha's Prescription for the End of Suffering

Buddha's great insight into the origin of human suffering can be seen as a monumental event that has transformed the course of our evolution. Buddha demonstrated spiritual genius in distilling his discovery into four simple and powerful noble truths, which have had profound global significance through the ages. Simply put, Buddha taught that human existential suffering—our individual and collective pathologies—arises from a fundamental flaw in how we use our minds, which distorts how we shape our selves, our world, and our living realities.

Buddha's enlightenment revealed that the egocentric patterns of our minds—*judgment* of others and *attachment* to cherished outcomes—are the origin of human pathologies. Buddha's profound prescription for humanity to remove this primal cause of human suffering is summed up in his Four Noble Truths. The principal way to end suffering is to recognize that egoic patterns of thinking directly cause our afflictions. We must become aware that our day-to-day reality is caused by how we use our minds, and we must learn to see clearly that our egocentric habits of mind can be terminated. We have a direct choice to break these negative habits and regenerate new integral patterns of the mind that bring us into alignment and harmony with our Selves and with each other. Buddha's Eightfold Path is precisely this prescription of how to break the old egocentric mind barriers and cross into a new life of awakened mind, or as the authors of this book would say, "Give up the story—of who you think you are."

Easier said than done. Twenty-five hundred years have passed since Buddha's great awakening, yet planetary history has shown us that we humans are still very much lodged in egocentric patterns of minding. We continue to follow chronic patterns of pathology, violence, and existential suffering. Furthermore, Buddha's deep diagnosis of the origins of human disorders in egocentric minding has been echoed and validated through the ages in an emergent global consensus of diverse spiritual technologies and worldviews. For when we stand back from privileging any one worldview or cultural lens, and cross into the higher global dimension where diverse mystical and experiential worldviews (such as Gnostic Christianity, kabbalistic Judaism, Sufism, and so on) co-originate, we can see that Buddha's findings are strongly vindicated.

Through this global lens, it is striking that our great spiritual, religious, and philosophical traditions concur that we humans cocreate our worlds through the conduct of our minds. Furthermore, our egocentric patterns produce fragmentations, dualisms, and existential alienation that generate all sorts of pathologies. So if it is, indeed, a global axiom that egocentric patterns of mind produce suffering, the obvious question is: Why has it been so difficult for us as individuals and as a species to overcome these egomind addictions and to rehabilitate our mind practices in more integral and healthful ways? Why do we continue to choose to suffer individually and collectively—perhaps now more than ever? Can we break through the egomind barrier?

Nagarjuna's Historic Breakthrough

The last question is all the more compelling in the light of the second-century Buddhist innovator's monumental breakthrough in bringing forth an unprecedented spiritual technology for finding the middle way to cross out of the bondage of egomind. Nagarjuna's new formulation of the Middle Way, the Madhyamika school, teaches that the sacred pathway leads beyond the egomind into the boundless open space of Buddha's *dharma* (moral law)— the infinite and spacious unified field of Reality. Nagarjuna found that early interpreters of Buddha's radical teaching remained caught up in the tangle of egocentric reasoning, and they fatally missed the essential teaching of Buddha's liberation.

While the genius of Buddha diagnosed clearly the origin of human pathologies in the egocentric habits of mind, and prescribed the philosophical therapy essential for rehabilitating the awakened mind, Nagarjuna's spiritual and philosophical genius saw precisely how and why we humans remain entrapped within deep and chronic egocentric habits. He built on Buddha's teaching by innovating an even more potent rational therapy for breaking the ego barrier and bringing to actualization this liberating teaching. In this respect, Nagarjuna stands out in global history as an unprecedented teacher of the highest order whose spiritual and rational innovations and technology deserve supreme acknowledgment and appropriate recognition.

Nevertheless, Nagarjuna's name remains virtually unknown on the global scene. His ingenious innovations are still not duly recognized or properly understood by the general public or our academic world. Still, what is most important here is not so much that Nagarjuna's name and work gain appropriate recognition. But rather, it is his clear and decisive teaching of entering the spacious Middle Way out of the bondage and suffering of egocentric mind that is more vital than ever for our individual and collective flourishing as one human family caring for each member.

The point is that Buddha's global truths are not just for "Buddhists," any more than Nagarjuna's spiritual technology for breaking the egomind barrier is for a select few on the Buddhist path. This teaching is meant for all humans, in all walks of life, of all worldviews and perspectives, who are caught in the force fields of egomind and are suffering the consequences.

That is why this book, *The End of Suffering*, by Russell Targ and J. J. Hurtak, is so vital for all readers at this time. The authors perform here a great service to humanity by making Nagarjuna's teaching on the end of suffering transparent and accessible to the general reader. They make his profound innovations available and relevant to our lives in today's world. And readers who enter this work will find powerful tools and insights that will empower them to get right to the source of their existential suffering. This important book fills a void and builds a bridge that helps make Buddha's global teachings and Nagarjuna's spiritual technology on the end of suffering a living reality for all who truly wish to help end individual and collective suffering in our human condition.

—Ashok Gangadean
Professor of Philosophy, Haverford College
Founder-Director of the Global Dialogue Institute
Co-convenor of the World Commission on
Global Consciousness and Spirituality
Author: *The Awakening of the Global Mind*
www.awakeningmind.org

Preface

by Russell Targ

Everybody suffers, yet most of this suffering is unnecessary—it can be overcome. Suffering results from our delusional cultural conditioning created by family, school, and television from which we create our personal story of who we think we are. From earliest times, it has been known that suffering can be transformed when we finally learn to change our minds.

Buddha's first great Truth identifies suffering as caused by our awareness of life's impermanence and fragility. I recognize that from time to time everyone experiences unavoidable pain, which I think of as naked suffering. This can come from intractable poverty, physical illness or injury, or from the grief and pain we feel over the loss of a loved one. Our heart breaks from the death of someone we deeply love or from the loss of a loving partner who simply decides to leave us. We experience these kinds of losses as tragedies in our hearts and in our lives. In fact, it was the untimely death of my beloved daughter and research buddy, Dr. Elisabeth Targ, that motivated me to start examining my own suffering. Such an examination was, no doubt, the natural way for me as a scientist to move through my own grieving process.

On the other hand, the suffering we address in this book—"the slings and arrows" that seem to attack our ego—what I call "our precious story"—is in essence nonexistent because it doesn't actually exist in present time where we live. Almost all of our suffering is in our mind: guilt or depression over things that have occurred in the past, or anxiety over things that might or might not happen in the future. Unless we happen to be in a concentration camp, our suffering almost always arises from a time frame not of the present, rather than from existential reality. We can carry in our memories anger, guilt, and especially resentment toward people who have mistreated or betrayed us even long after those nasty people have departed or died. But we can also choose to empty this mental backpack instead of lugging around our treasured old garbage. We cling to this garbage because it is part of our story—who we believe we are. Our social environment continually and pervasively conditions us to harbor grudges, to feel resentment, fear, guilt, and revenge, and above all to express judgment about everyone and everything. These learned behaviors cause suffering principally to us, but also to others. It is a well-known psychological dynamic that the more we judge other people, the more we are unhappy ourselves. So why do we continue to behave in ways that cause us suffering? The explanation is not simple and represents the main body of this book. Based on the authors' experience, however, we propose that it is not difficult to learn to consciously transcend fear, resentment, and desperation for a life of gratitude, peace, and love—if that's what the individual would like to experience.

We create the conditioned suffering by our desire to defend our stories—our business cards so to speak—and *our picture of who we think we are.* On television recently, I watched a young prisoner dressed in detainee orange explain to the judge, "I had to shoot him. He disrespected me." It was as though he had no idea of what else he could have done at that moment.

Several years ago, I was offering to rent a spare room in my Palo Alto home to Stanford graduate students. An attractive woman in her late twenties came to look at the room. By the time she finished writing her rent check, I had learned not only that she was earning a doctoral degree in clinical psychology, but also that as a teenager she had been sexually abused by her father. As a landlord, I didn't really need to know this information; however, from her point of view, it would define for me *who she was!* The fact that she was abused was a major plot point in her story. She had become *attached and comfortable* with her suffering and victimhood. Even a decade later, as an adult graduate student, she was still suffering as an abused teenager. That's what we mean by one's story.

The hidden craziness underlying the conditioned behavior that makes us suffer is the dualistic, "either-or" mode of thinking we have been immersed in since childhood. And it is all Aristotle's influence. Aristotle defined a profoundly dualistic system that he called the "law of the excluded middle," which asserts that everything in the world is either black or it's not black, thereby excluding any other possibilities. This kind of dualistic thinking is what makes political propagandists such as President Bush say things like "those who are not with us are with the terrorists," ignoring the huge majority of the world that sees other possibilities. The propagandist's goal is to make us feel fearful. With a yellow alert we are told to feel pretty fearful, and with an orange alert we should feel very fearful, while always watching out for "doomsday red." But there is an important middle ground between fearfulness and complacency. The middle ground we seek is not a case of either-or, this or that; the middle ground is vigilance and the fearlessness to experience the situation as it is. Given the choice, our goal is to choose fearlessness and freedom every time.

Most things we read or encounter in life are neither true nor not true. For example, physicists know it is true that the light we see is neither a wave nor a particle but can manifest as either. Also, who we truly are as conscious beings is neither physical nor not physical. The so-called wave-particle paradox and the famous mind-body duality are both examples of incorrectly posed questions, confusingly masquerading as dichotomies. Think of the well-known "glass half-full or half-empty" metaphor . . . What if it's neither?

Our usual black-and-white dualistic frame of mind almost inevitably creates suffering for ourselves and others because we seriously misperceive reality, polarizing it into incommensurable opposites, and therefore we experience delusion. But once we learn to shed our conditioned awareness and move our consciousness to what the Buddhists call naked existence, we are finally able to experience our lives free of our habitual conditioning.

This nondual understanding of reality was perfected by Nagarjuna, the second-century Indian genius and teacher of the "Middle Way," whom the Dalai Lama described as one of the truly enlightened people of all time. The Middle Way is a very generous path that runs brilliantly between dogmatic, materialistic absolutism and insubstantial nihilism (where nothing means anything). It teaches that ignorance of who we really are and attachment to materiality are at the root of our suffering.

The Middle Way is not to be confused with the newly developed "fuzzy logic" loved by computer scientists, which simply explores a linear range of possibilities for a statement that can run from true to false in arbitrary little steps. Instead, Nagarjuna explored another dimension of possibilities. He taught that as we go through our lives, we give all the meaning there is to everything we experience. In other words, our experience is almost entirely subjective (or projective). This is why different people will have such strikingly different responses to the same event, picture, food, or performance. The Buddhists would say that nothing at all is happening, except to the extent that we assign our personal meaning to it—and that we have the freedom to make such a decision. Shakespeare knew this when he had Hamlet say, "There is nothing either good or bad, but thinking makes it so" (Act II, Scene 2).

The Vinegar Story

Long, long ago, the Buddha was strolling through the sands of time along the Ganges River. He spied an earthenware jar and pulled it from the riverbank. He opened the jar and tasted what was inside. It was extremely bitter and sour. It represented a potential source of great suffering to the world so he poured it out on the ground.

Five hundred years later, Jesus of Nazareth was meditating in the desert near Galilee. As he pitched his tent, he came upon an earthenware jar buried in the sand. Opening the jar, he tasted the bitter and sour contents, and thought they represented great potential suffering for the world so he drank them all himself.

Last year, two lovers were strolling along the beautiful beach at Santa Barbara. As they were putting down their blanket for a picnic, they came upon the same little earthenware jar buried in the sand. They opened the bottle, tasted the liquid inside, and spent the entire warm afternoon licking the delicious drops from each other's fingertips.

We have the opportunity to give all the meaning there is to everything we experience. That is, we must learn to *question reality*. Each day we have the choice to defend our ego and relive our story, or we can find a way to choose differently, give up dualistic thinking, and reside in love. That's the choice we explore in this book.

"Hey, pal, do you have any idea who I think I am?"

Acknowledgments

First and foremost, we want to give great and heartfelt thanks to our wives, Patricia Kathleen Targ and Desiree Hurtak, for their very significant and thoughtful contributions to every phase of this book, from concept and contents to editing and proofreading.

In addition, I (Russell) want to thank Gangaji for her transmission of spiritual guiding light, which led me out of the darkness. She stood as an exemplar at the time that I most needed inspiration and guidance. At this very late date, I want to thank and recognize my first spiritual teacher, Mollie May Butler Maragliotti, who found me as a 20-year-old graduate student in the physics department at Columbia University, where she was working as a draftsman in the highest loft at Pupin Hall. She took me to meetings at the New York Theosophical Society and introduced me to Dora Kunz, a great spiritual healer, psychic practitioner, and president of the society. This was my first introduction to the teachings of Vedanta and Buddhism. Thank you, Mollie, for seeing the soul in the baby physicist. Thirty years later, when I was recovering from cancer surgery, Mollie found me in a California hospital to send me a copy of her dissertation on the great second-century genius Nagarjuna, who is the subject of this book. I also want to thank Judith Skutch Whitson for giving me a first edition of *A Course in Miracles* as it was hot off the press; and for her always sage advice and continuing support and love.

And finally, I want to express my appreciation to Frank DeMarco, my editor and publisher, for having faith in this book in spite of its difficult moments, and giving me the opportunity to share the wisdom of Nagarjuna.

In the spirit of unity between East and West, North and South, I (J. J. Hurtak) would also like to thank my students throughout the world who have given their life in service to humanity by discovering that global consciousness comes from the exploration of the inner self. Let this little book remind us that humankind is blessed with the gift of consciousness as the reflection of God on earth. We are part of a greater design which we will discover in our earnest search for the meaning and unfoldment of Life. Let us realize that the "Day of Graduation" (*Yom Or*) is daily before us as we begin to use our greater Love.

PART ONE

The End of Suffering

1

Why Do We Suffer?

If we have no peace, it is because we have forgotten we belong to each other.

—Mother Teresa

Suffering is part of the human condition. It comes from our own existence as separate bodies that react to our emotions and our rational mind. The principal cause of suffering is attachment. This is the Buddha's basic teaching of the Four Noble Truths.[1] We crave and desire fulfillment from people, places, and things, and we strive for cherished outcomes in the so-called external world. We learn to fear life's impermanence; thus we cling to things that are in themselves impermanent. This clinging to ever-changing externalities, rooted mainly in our personal story, results in our experienced separation from one another and from the Truth or the Divine.

Our sense of separation causes suffering by leading us to search for love or the experience of the Divine outside the Self, just as in Marc Almond's well-known song "Looking for Love in All the Wrong Places." As his lyrics state, "Learn to love yourself before anyone else." In the movie *On the Waterfront,* Marlon Brando cries out poignantly, "I could have been a contender. I could have been *somebody.*" That's what we all long for—the discovery of who we are. I (Targ) was once talking about Buddhist traditions with a group of Nashville songwriters. I described the familiar teaching that "the love we are looking for is already within us." They agreed, but laughed and said that if this idea gets out, no one will listen to popular songs, whose main theme is "the IFD disease—idealization, frustration (because the ideal can never be found), and demoralization."[2] This is the same path through life that the philosopher Arthur Schopenhauer describes as "striving, disappointment, and boredom"—utterly devoid of any internal spiritual life.

In his book on the Enneagram, psychologist and spiritual teacher Eli Jaxon-Bear makes this important idea touchingly clear. He writes:

> When identification shifts from a particular body . . . to the totality of all being, the soul realizes itself as pure limitless consciousness. This shift in identification is called Self-realization. In this realization, not only do you find that love is all there is, *but you also discover that this love is who you are.*[3] [emphasis added]

The Hindu Vedas and other scriptures teach the critically

important idea that *we already have within ourselves the love and everything else we could possibly want.* Pema Chödrön, Buddhist teacher and student of Chögyam Trungpa Rinpoche, describes this as "the dynamic energy of the awakened heart." And the Gospel of Luke confirms that "the kingdom of God is within you." As physicist and writer Peter Russell says, "Love is the secret sensation of the Self." Yet love is clearly more than just a feeling. It is a unifying experience and is spoken of as such in many of the world's scriptures.

One of the oldest and most profound truths is the Vedic teaching that *Atman* (the divine spirit or awareness within us) equals—is one with—*Brahman* (the whole undivided physical and nonphysical universe). This equality of Atman and Brahman is also a precursor of the twentieth-century physics discovery of nonlocality and our nonlocal awareness. In physics, nonlocality means that particles are connected with each other, or entangled, even though they are moving away from each other at the speed of light. This entanglement is inherent in the very nature of the space and time in which we live. The experience of nonlocal or spacious awareness is the gateway to the love and liberation that *lead to discovery of who we really are.* Spaciousness of mind and nonattachment to stuff allow us to expand our awareness to experience oceanic connections with all of nature. It is the pristine mirror that leads to what Jesus called *"the peace that passes understanding."* Spaciousness is an expression of unbounded love that allows our awareness to fill the interconnected universe. And the Buddha describes the end of suffering in which we are finally liberated to experience the world with naked awareness instead of with the conditioned awareness of grasping, judgment, resentment, and the fear of impermanence. One could say that enlightenment is the state in which we experience everything for the first time; that is, our lives are a succession of many awakened moments of pure naked awareness.

Suffering, the Buddha taught, is caused when the freedom that is inherent to our nonlocal pristine awareness is obscured by the limitations of our ego and our physical body. We forget that we are pure awareness, residing only for a time as a physical body. This does not mean that we should ignore our body. Bodies, we are told, are very precious and hard to come by; they are the seats of emotions, without which we would be missing our empathetic connections with one another. Emotions are ubiquitous guides, leading to wisdom along the path; thus the body is a valuable teacher. We are, however, more than just a body.

Most of us begin life with total love for and acceptance of the world around us, but as we grow older we learn to constrict these feelings in response to the unpredictable experiences of life. We experience both good and bad, and the meaning of these experiences is not always clear to us. We get caught up in the daily game of scripting and role-playing. We dramatize our ego, which is the story of who we think we are. Our so-called business card is really our story card. The more we think that our story, accomplishments, and recognition represent all that we are, the more we suffer, because it's not the truth.

Of course, many of us try to move beyond reinventing ourselves externally—new clothes, new car, new face, new partner. Still, the powerful inner need for self-realization and the apparent lack of love around us can make life seem almost unbearable. And confusing your story with your true nature leads to unsustainable inner contradiction and paradox. The actress Marilyn Monroe was an outstanding example of this problem— a person who seemed to have everything—and nothing, not even a self. In spite of her beauty, wealth, and position, she became lost in the Marilyn Monroe persona of her own creation. As she walked the alluring and profitable tightrope between innocence and sexuality, she was, in the end, unable to internalize and discover the woman behind all the photos. For Marilyn, being seduced by her story produced negative thoughts that began to outweigh her positive appreciation of life. It was this dissonance of story versus life that made her both crazy and sick. Over a long period of time, these contradictory thoughts, whether we are conscious of them or not, can become disruptive forces that bring *dis-ease* to our minds and our bodies.

Equally as important as surrendering one's story is not to expect or crave applause—or even thanks. If you or I have done the job to the best of our ability, we don't really need the standing ovation. If you want a reward, then Saint Matthew suggests saying your prayers and doing your good deeds in secret (until the desire for reward passes). It's the hypocrite who prays loudly on the street corner and puts the Ten Commandments on the front lawn, to paraphrase Matthew 6:5–6. The hypocrite confuses the experience with the form.

Disruptive forces abound. We live primarily in a world of competition, acquisition, and consumption. Living with television, e-mail, cell phones, and the Internet, we rarely experience a single quiet moment. Constant exposure to television and other media places a tremendous amount of emphasis on who we "should be," which can lead to depression becoming a "normal" part of life. In his epic book on contemporary shamanism, Daniel Pinchbeck writes, "We live in a world of data overload and media smog, where everything distracts from everything else. Yet underlying this noisy assault, our culture offers us nothing transcendent. No deeper meaning, no abiding hope."[4] The goal of advertising is to make us feel unhappy and needy and then promise relief. *Its purpose is to create suffering* that can be relieved only by purchasing a product that will fulfill a need that we never knew we had. Living in a multimedia environment, we are also exposed to a dehumanizing atmosphere, where we build up a tolerance, even an indifference, to the violence and hardship experienced by others. We begin to view the televised suffering of others as separate from ourselves, as though this media saturation has overloaded our "empathy chip."

Although we all experience suffering in our lives, many people store up their emotional pains and resentments—suppressing instead of expressing their feelings and emotions. Others act out the pain through anger and rage without being aware of the root cause. Whether repressing or acting out, our culture spends millions of dollars on psychologists and psychiatrists, often without ever fully exploring the "fundamentals" of why we are not happy. Quieting our minds is never easy and is certainly more difficult without deeper levels of awareness and inner development to determine the source of our suffering.

Whenever peace tries to be present, chaos also attempts to gain control. For example, you have just finished your meditation, then you turn on the radio and hear a terrible news report about this group killing that group. It is essential that we overcome the ubiquitous and poisonous "us versus them" mentality fostered by the media. Each of us can break out of our dualistic worldview by changing the way we think and act in relation to each other. We will be happier if we work together as a collective force, because we are all one in consciousness.

Exploration of life can transcend the illusions of a separate self trying to find answers in the material world, where money can never buy the love or the happiness we are seeking. We cannot relieve suffering by replacing one ego-centered story with another—or seeking another "I" outside ourselves to find fulfillment. The idea that I am a pretty good half-a-person seeking a similarly fractional partner to complete me is never successful. This creates an unhealthy codependence that frequently leads to resentment when the other half quits doing whatever he or she did to make me feel whole. This is why codependent love can so quickly turn to hatred. When the other half-a-person, or some material thing, does not fulfill our needs, we convince ourselves that we are indeed alone, believing that nobody understands our pain or fears. This situation often leads people to explore alcohol or drugs to relieve their pain. The point is, by transcending the illusion of a separate self, you can contact your own loving nature *before* you start searching for a partner to travel with you on a spiritual path.

With only a small change in perception, we can release ourselves from our constrictive space of personal isolation and from feeling that we are victims of circumstance. For example, we can begin to perceive that *we give all the meaning there is to everything we experience.* This is why we hear that "The coward dies a thousand deaths" (of the ego). We all have the power to take back control of our lives and experience our higher selves rather than just have things happen to us. When we are stopped in traffic, for instance, we can pound the steering wheel and experience our ego reacting with impatience and anger, or we can welcome the opportunity to slow down and appreciate our surroundings or spend a moment in gratitude. This teaching is another example of the very important Buddhist teaching on *emptiness (sunyata),* where nothing at all is happening, except for the meaning we assign to it. This is one of the many strong parallels between Buddhism and the twentieth-century spiritual guide called *A Course in Miracles.* Also, there is a

Buddhist newspaper, called *The Dot,* whose motto is "Nothing happens, and we report it."

Developing compassion is a step on the path to the end of suffering. From this perspective, Western philosophers like Kierkegaard and Pascal argued that good works come only from suffering and the pressures of life, and that greatness derives from grief and pain, poverty, destitution, and a thousand other obstructions. The great East European mystic of the last century, Gurdjieff, also speaks about *voluntary suffering,* which is when we choose to bear the unpleasant manifestations of others. Difficult relatives are the usual opportunity for this practice. Acknowledging difficulties is a spiritual exercise to recognize the ego, which wants to strike back or push away, instead of remaining centered in the face of unpleasant inner turmoil. This is similar to the Buddhist *tonglen* practice, the meditation practice of sending and receiving, in which you give away all your joy and goodness with each outbreath, then take in resentment and foulness of the world with each inbreath. The objective of all the practices is to let go of attachments and develop compassion and lovingkindness for yourself and others. Compassion is the key. Letting go of attachment does not mean disinterest. Our goal here—that which gives meaning to our lives—is to understand and experience the truth, and then to share that open-hearted and unitive experience with others. Meditation is the path providing the mind-quieting opportunity to practice what Pema Chödrön calls the four Limitless Qualities of lovingkindness, compassion, joy, and equanimity.[5]

There is, however, genuine suffering connected with profound sadness and grief that we feel in our heart, for example, from the loss of a child or loved one. Often crisis causes a complete change in our reality structure, which can bring us to the point of *paradigm shift*. The shift that occurs as a result of suffering can lead us to the experience of love and compassion—the oceanic connection to nature and all life. Compassion, love, and the experience and understanding of egolessness are essential ingredients that facilitate the end of suffering. Nonjudgmental emptiness is a primary requirement for true compassion.

For the most part, our everyday suffering is not caused by tragic events of the heart, but rather by insults—real or imagined—to our ego story. Suffering is the response to these imagined attacks that interfere with what we want and what we feel we need. Fortunately, we can learn to let go of these conditioned responses and view suffering as a delusional idea. We can choose not to collect suffering memorabilia to paste into our scrapbooks. Since our personal story is only made up of *ideas,* we can learn to release these ego-insults and let them float away like helium balloons. Or, as Ken Wilber would say, if you don't want to suffer, "ditch the small self." We the authors would say, "Give up the story—the story of ME."

We are spiritually asleep if we allow the regrets of the past, the worries and fears of the future, and the expectation of others to guide our lives. In the midst of the panicky feelings and beliefs and the distractions of this spiritual sleep, it is most difficult to summon intuition or to hear the voice of inner wisdom. The combination of guilt from the past and fear of the future prevents us from experiencing the present. This projection is what Dzogchen Buddhists call *conditioned awareness,* and it profoundly interferes with the *timeless existence* we are describing in this book.

With regard to fear of the future and guilt over the past, the great screenwriter and director Woody Allen has made a career out of his lifelong suffering. In a recent *Associated Press* interview, he describes his view of life:

Most of life is tragic. You're born, you don't know why. You're here, you don't know why. You go, you die. Your family dies. Your friends die. People suffer. People live in constant terror. The world is full of poverty and corruption and war and Nazis and tsunamis. . . .[6]

This is New York existential angst, where basically everything sucks. This stance, however, has served Woody very well—through several Academy Awards and more than 20 nominations. Of course, we notice that much of his suffering is either in the past or in the future. He is not presently in pain, as far as we know.

Elie Wiesel, who survived the Holocaust and several concentration camps and went on to win a Nobel Peace Prize, admonished a Jewish writer friend on the subject of forgiveness. He said you should never be silent, but that if you don't let go of hating the Nazis, then they have won and you are still in the camp.

If we were to begin talking with Woody Allen, we would invite him to the Stage Delicatessen on Seventh Avenue. And after he had bitten into a big fat corned beef sandwich, with the juice dripping off his chin, we would ask him to tell us about his suffering. We would respectfully investigate whether it is possible to get him to focus his brilliant mind on the present moment where nothing at all is happening but sandwiches. Or are we doomed to forever share our table with Nazis and death?

This kind of conditioned awareness pertains to the beliefs we hold about every aspect of our life, but they are merely artificial constructs—not reality. As our belief system moves into naked unconditioned awareness, we ourselves become more spacious, expanding our awareness beyond the ego-centered self to a new discernment of what is real and what is not. Once released from our mental prison, we can see that we have held rigid concepts of what we are, biologically and socially, and about how we think of time, matter, and existence. Although our wounds and betrayals can give rise to certain levels of judgment and resentment, our goal is to give them up and be more in tune with our positive emotions, and also to nurture gratitude, compassion, and love.

We are connected to one another and that is why we love. We learn to view ourselves as one in consciousness, rather than as entirely separate individuals. The ability to love leads to the awareness that we are more than just a body. This awareness is a *transformation* of consciousness; it is not a *transcendence* to a different plane of existence. Of course, the surrendering of judgment of others does not mean we give up our discernment in separating reality from illusion. If the ancient classical thinkers were correct—that nature is a source of guidance for human behavior—then surely science as the study of nature should also concern itself with showing us what is wise or unwise in our relationship to one another.

Notes

1. Buddha's Four Noble Truths come to us from 500 B.C. India. The First Noble Truth is indisputable: We experience pain because we are aware of the fragile, finite, temporary nature of our lives. The Second Noble Truth addresses the additional suffering caused by craving and attachment. The Third Noble Truth offers the terrific good news that when we take control of our free-running, chattering minds, we have the opportunity to exchange suffering for gratitude. And the Fourth Noble Truth describes the Buddhist Eightfold Path of the right view of right living, which leads to the end of suffering we describe later.

2. S. I. Hayakawa, "Popular songs vs. the facts of life," *Etc.* (Winter 1955), pp. 85–95.

3. Eli Jaxon-Bear, *The Enneagram of Liberation: From Fixation to Freedom*, Stinson Beach, CA: Leela Foundation, 2002.

4. Daniel Pinchbeck, *Breaking Open the Head: A Psychedelic Journey into the Heart of Contemporary Shamanism*, New York: Broadway Books, 2002, p. 16.

5. Pema Chödrön, *Comfortable with Uncertainty*, Boston: Shambhala, 2002, p. 5.

6. Douglas J. Rowe, "Interview with Woody Allen," *San Jose Mercury News* (March 26, 2005), p. E3.

2

Our Limited View of Ourselves: Duality and Two-Valued Logic as a Cause of Suffering

Aristotle's goal, around 350 B.C., was to codify the essential nature of science by defining its forms and laws—inspired by his teacher, Plato. He also introduced linguistic structures that began the foundation of Western civilization—the study of logic. His plan was to define objective reality by expounding on what we label "objects," things having their own reality outside our apprehension of them. Aristotle taught that objects have inherent properties and that they manifest these properties in the physical world independent of the observer. Until quite recently, Western civilization has exclusively used Aristotelian two-valued (A, or not A) logical objective orientation. In two-valued logic, the world is either eternal, or it is not eternal—not both. Aristotle called this the "law of the excluded middle." Something being true or not true (A, or not A) is a corollary of the idea of independent existence and identity.

As we shall learn from both quantum physics and Nagarjuna, however, the observer is not independent, but always affects the observed. The important Buddhist teaching of *sunyata* (emptiness) also informs us that things are empty of inherent meaning and have only the meaning we give them. This means that they cannot have the independent existence that Aristotle declared. This is the Buddhist principle of mutual coarising—like the mutual and simultaneous appearance of a magnetic field whenever one has a propagating or time-varying electric field. A lightning strike, as well as a comb pulled through your hair, generates both a magnetic field and an electrical spark. Similarly, in modern relativistic physics, Einstein taught that there can be no space without matter and no time without events for time to delineate. Time and space, gravity and inertia, and the Buddhist karma are all examples of what we mean by mutual coarising.

Since Aristotelian logic focuses mainly on externalized observation of "facts" and "figures," when this system is applied to the individual, a split takes place between the "I" and the "other," as we shall see. The two-valued Aristotelian "law of the excluded middle," with the resulting split, provided a logical institutionalized basis for millions of human beings to exist as slaves, entrapped by intellectual and emotional constructs. The law of the excluded middle is the law of separation. As we have seen through the ages, this structured dualism is the idea that "everyone who isn't with us is against us."

If someone makes a remark to you about your performance or appearance, you have several choices as to how you might react, or what you might experience. You could tell them straightaway what they can do with their nasty comment. That usually feels good for a moment. Or you could repress your resentment and paste it into your resentment scrapbook. But there actually is a middle ground between acting out and repressing. It is called "letting go" and experiencing your own open-hearted and energetic flow of loving awareness. Although someone said "Boo!" nothing is actually happening beyond the meaning you give it. This is just one example of why we (the authors) are passionate about exploring and learning to live in the usually excluded middle.

Slavery was the rule in ancient Athens, as well as in Europe and America. Slavery could exist only in a separatist and dualistic culture of "self versus other." There are "us Greek men," then there are the others, including women and slaves. From the Greeks' radical idealization of men came machismo and paternalism, as well as the general acceptance of slavery and oppression of the other. Two-valued logic gives rise to lack of empathy and fear of the other, whether it manifests as a Christian Crusade, an Islamic Jihad, or plain old-fashioned Western imperialism with its extermination of indigenous people. For example, Pope Pius XII successfully saved German cripples from Nazi euthanasia because they were largely Christians. But he expended no such effort to save millions of German Jews and gypsies because they were "the other."

Daniel Mendelsohn, in the *New York Times* magazine, recently wrote on this subject of the Greek ego and duality in an article entitled "What Olympic Ideal?":

> Whereas today's Olympic committee prefers to "celebrate humanity" (an official slogan of contemporary Olympiads), the [ancient] Greek athlete wanted only to be celebrated himself; it was his one ticket to immortality.

It is difficult for us today to conceive of the extent to which a ferocious competitiveness fueled so much of Greek culture, virtually no aspect of which was not somehow organized into a competition. This all-consuming egotism at the heart of the Greek motivation sits ill at ease with the notion that you must love your neighbor as yourself. But then, the attempt to graft the modern Olympics onto the ancient ones was awkward from the start. (August 8, 2004, p. 11)

A dramatically dualistic worldview inherently leads to suffering. It has done so for millennia in religions that have the self-appointed task of creating separation between us and experience of the divine. This is equally true in politics, economics, and human relations, all of which are organized in a hierarchical power structure. In a dualistic system, there are fewer options. For example, even in our contemporary Judeo-Christian institutions, two-valued logic is built in. We have a powerful—even omnipotent—deity way out there, and a puny little self (me) down here. This construct of thought has the effect of separating us from our divine nature by projecting our searching elsewhere and is the idolatry we are warned against in the Ten Commandments. Idolatry implies separation, and the idea that there is an omnipotent "god" out there is an idolatrous idea. There is, in fact, no separation.

In the more expansive and inclusive (neither A nor not A) four-valued logic description of nondual realities, the world is neither eternal nor not eternal. The glass is neither half-empty nor half-full. A profoundly nondual view says that you and the deity are inseparable. Jesus tells us in the recently discovered Gospel of Thomas (Chapter 22), "When you make two into one, and when you make the inner like the outer, and the outer like the inner, the upper like the lower, and when you make male and female into one . . . then you will enter the [Father's] domain"—unifying you with all there is, it is who you are! Poets, mystics, and composers experience this and can show us this experience of the divine, which is both nondual and nonconceptual. Our effort in this book is to bring this transcendent reality defined as ineffable into the realm of rational discourse.

For more than two thousand years, the human nervous system in the Western world has been ensnared in the restrictive, oppressive, often delusional orientations of dualism, which is reflected in the very structure of the language we habitually use. The word "divine" comes to us from the Sanskrit *diva,* which is a name for God, whereas the word "devil" comes from the Sanskrit word for division *(dvaidha).* So the devil is the root idea behind all dualistic thought. In Hebrew, "Satan" has the Aramaic root *sta,* meaning the slipping away or the causing of separation, more commonly known as the adversary, divider, or enemy. The "devil" or "Satan" is that which divides or separates us from our divinity, from each other, and from Nature.

The devil has no more independent existence than does evil. Saying that it does is like saying there are two forces in the world: cold and heat. In fact, there is only heat and the absence of heat, energy and the absence of energy, light and the absence of light. It is logically incoherent to speak of anything as a source of darkness. Darkness cannot be the source of anything, let alone the often-heard idea that "the devil made me do it." Evil is not a separate entity simply existing out there. Satan represents the loss of our inherent goodness or not using our divine abilities. We the authors contend that such divisions and separations are the source of most human suffering.

The destruction of the World Trade Center on September

11, 2001, was the result of the collective thoughts and actions of Eastern and Western societies for many centuries, exemplifying the egoism, misunderstanding, and separation of religious and political institutions. It would be absurd to say that the catastrophe was due to actions on a single day and to neglect our shared responsibility in creating this planetary force—a horrific and indisputable example of mutual coarising.

Aristotle and many of the Greeks took the concept of separation to the extreme. In this strong expression of two-valued logic, men were everything and women were nothing. Older men sought to identify themselves with "youth." Homosexuality was one of the celebrated paths of education and transcendence. Yet we encounter in such relationships another kind of multivalued perspective, where a person could be "a man, and not a man." He might have had male body parts, but his self-image, worldview, and orientation were not considered entirely masculine. And women in this ancient Greek cradle of democracy were not citizens, could not vote, own property, or even leave their homes! They were defined as the other and completely separated from the dominant male culture.

Whenever you have a totally male-dominated system, there will be distortions in relationships. We see this today in the Catholic Church, which is run entirely by unmarried men and in which women have no authority. Could this separation have led in part to the ecclesiastical disaster of the sexual involvements of hundreds of priests that we read about almost daily?

Nonduality

The Pythagorean mystery school of the sixth century B.C. taught compassion and nonduality in Greek times, so ideas beyond a two-valued logic are not entirely culturally bound. Similarly, in pre-Christian times (sixth century B.C.), Lao Tsu, the great Chinese master of the Tao, also taught nonduality and created the yin and yang image as a powerful and enduring symbolic representation of male and female nonseparation, in which each aspect contains a significant representation of the other—neither is entirely male or female.

One of the earliest representations of nonduality

Yet, to this day, we have not transcended dualistic concepts. Consider the unbounded exploitation of dualistic capitalism, as a result of which we are experiencing a technocratic class-based society, wage slavery, and a present ecological crisis that could lead to planetary catastrophe. Similarly, much of today's suffering can be attributed to powerful men dominating the poor and weak, especially women. This is possible only in a two-valued dualistic society that seeks to identify specifics and ignore the interconnected whole. In economics, there is no identification with the people who are being exploited. For example, in modern society, we observe the outrageous spectacle of corporations paying managers a thousand times more than their workers. In science, two-valued logic leads to reductionism where a thing is exactly equal to the sum of its parts and the holistic relationship is neglected. That is, the doctor sees *that* you have cancer with no concern for *why* you have cancer.

How Do Thoughts Cause Suffering?

Suffering comes from mistaking our mental representation of reality for Reality itself—as in the pioneering non-Aristotelian semanticist Alfred Korzybski's famous teaching that "the map is not the territory."[1] He taught that nothing is black and white, that the period at the end of a sentence stands for "et cetera"— all the other things that haven't been said. Differences between the orders of abstraction include differences between verbal and nonverbal levels, between descriptions and inferences, and (especially) between my abstractions and your abstractions, et cetera. On the path to alleviate suffering, we begin by exploring our beliefs. What beliefs are we holding? What beliefs do we refuse to let go? Letting go of our cherished beliefs is a lot harder than it sounds, because we may not be aware of all our beliefs and premises. Many of them are so fundamental that we have forgotten we even have them. Ayn Rand, the well-known writer and intellectual of the twentieth century, knew this when she would tell her students, if you're still suffering, "check your premises"—and choose again.

Our thoughts noticeably affect our body. Thoughts and feelings in our brain create various neuropeptides that travel throughout the body to affect organs and our immune system. Suffering caused by unpleasant and uncontrollable thoughts and circumstances is one of our strongest emotions and can create some of the greatest harm to our physical body as well as to others, if it is not channeled properly.

The Mind-Body Connection

Candace Pert, research professor at Georgetown University Medical Center and author of *Molecules of Emotion,* tells us that, with physical and emotional stress, actual changes in the body can and do occur.[2] Emotional stress from suffering or negative thoughts can produce a sense of despair or hopelessness, which is mediated by the limbic system via the hypothalamus and, in turn, triggers suppression of the immune system. Some neuropeptides act as chemical messengers, communicating with our emotions. Since we know that everything is energy, we can conclude that there is no significant difference between the body's energy and the mind's energy. The specific importance of Pert's data is that our perceptions of information coming to us from the "outside" environment can directly suppress our immune system, make us sick, and kill us.

Dualistic thinking, which is created by our societal conditioning—media, parents, school, and so forth—can produce suffering. The potency of bad thoughts can cause misperceptions that result in the experience of emotional suffering—unstable emotions that boil up inside and create states of depression and illness. This is an example of the body as teacher. In discovering our greater Self, or wisdom mind, we gain the ability to maintain balance in order to alleviate mental suffering as well as physical suffering. We know when to assert ourselves and when to remain calm. We learn to let go of attachment to cherished outcomes and create space for our higher wisdom. By simply paying attention to here and now, we can surrender the small self and begin the process of letting go and discovering the Divine spaciousness, joy, and peace within.

Complete healing of the body and relief from suffering in the mind cannot be attained until we live and participate in a more self-aware conscious universe. But where do we begin? How do we break the cycle of fear and injustice—without feeling overwhelmed by them—and begin the process of discovering who we really are? If we can manage to change our focus and perception to the present moment, we see that our first real power lies in *an understanding of who we are* and why we are here. We will see that we truly have a purpose and can transmute feelings of suffering and fear into acts of positive love and optimum health, regardless of our circumstances in life.

Thus the challenge before us is to "rise to the occasion" and overcome those moments of fear, anger, and doubt. While some have chosen certain well-known chemical compounds called entheogens—LSD, MDMA (called "ecstasy"), ayahuasca, mescaline in peyote, or psilocybin in mushrooms—to experience the Divine and alleviate suffering, it can be successfully (and legally) accomplished through meditation practice, introspection, listening to sacred music, learning from a powerful teacher, or the practice of tantric yoga. Others may choose the path of transcendent sex. I, Targ, have considered that all these powerful technologies can lead to investigation of the ego and to the life-changing experience of oceanic oneness, spaciousness, connection to the Divine, and stopping our mental chatter.

Ultimately, it is our life's purpose to first feel ourselves as part of a deep unitive experience, and then to help others have that same experience. Through this, we can discover who we really are—which is that we are one with the Divine. According to Rabbi Lawrence Kushner, "God is a verb"—an activity taking place in consciousness—not a "being" separate from ourselves. Don't expect God to end your suffering.

A principal healing aid available to everyone is forgiveness, the releasing of our deeply rooted negative emotions by changing the way we think. It's definitely worth a try! This process usually begins with sending love and forgiveness to those closest to us who may have hurt us, even in the distant past; then we extend that love and forgiveness to all humanity. This process helps us to take control of our emotions and stop having them control us. By doing this, we can free ourselves of negative thoughts and feelings about others and ourselves, and awaken our understanding of fellowship or unconditional love.

We begin to discover that the principal source of pain and suffering is our feeling of isolation and sense of separation from meaning and from the Divine. We can never actually be separated from God, because we are not divisible from the feeling of spaciousness and joy. The sense of separation is an illusion of our own making. So, if we are suffering, we must learn to change our mind. The real source of our suffering is almost never external. All mystics hold this view. The evidence we have comes from the best possible source—direct personal experience. We can further expand our awareness of reality by opening our mind to the inclusive thought system suggested by Nagarjuna. We can escape the vicissitudes of traditional dualistic thinking and experience our nonlocal awareness and the Divine.

We need to begin to contemplate how our dualistic Aristotelian thought system causes suffering by giving rise to misunderstandings, false dichotomies, and the belief that ego is the real deal; then we can begin to expand our thinking from dualism to a more inclusive thought system. An expanded logic can help us break ego boundaries and experience pure awareness. The purpose of this book is to help orient the reader to loving the Self unconditionally and, in so doing, loving and respecting the right to life of all natural beings, finding relief from suffering, and experiencing inner peace. Ultimately, one is to awaken within oneself a conscious new being that no longer denies the existence of a greater mental, emotional, and spiritual unity. By removing the so-called conflicts, one realizes harmony and an end to suffering. What we are talking about here is self-realization, much more than self-improvement.

Notes

1. Alfred Korzybski, *Science and Sanity: An Introduction to Non-Aristotelian Systems and General Semantics*, Fort Worth, TX: Institute for General Semantics, 1995.

2. Candace Pert, *Molecules of Emotion: The Science behind Mind-Body Medicine*, New York: Scribner, 1999.

3

Looking beyond Aristotle: Freedom and Nonduality in Language and Thought

Reality for us is what we experience. And since we are conditioned to perceive using Aristotelian logic, we've become stuck in a dualistic reality. Our Western language structure is rooted in Aristotelian logic. Neither words nor sentences allow for flexibility of abstract thought outside a dualistic framework. In fact, it is this limitation of language that makes it so difficult to describe nonconceptual nondual reality. By its very nature, the historical semantics of Aristotelian-based thought prohibits semantic and linguistic development beyond the two-valued construct of "he said black, and she said white." Our language doesn't allow for shades of gray. It is like our legal system; it can allow verdicts only of guilty or not guilty. We must create room for grayness, to say nothing of a little color.

Two-valued logic provides a linear one-dimensional view of reality with clearly defined boundaries of who you are and who everyone else is. But if you view everyone else as separate and yourself as an isolated individual, your thoughts and thinking quickly become anchored in materiality and physicality, and you lose awareness of your precious spacious nature. The result can be a lack of empathy and a focus completely on the self. In this *self-absorption,* one has the strong tendency to think only of the physical needs of the body—I need a house, a car, a better job, sex, or whatever thing it may be. When the focus of attention is on the acquisition of what you do not (apparently) have, then you find yourself squarely in the box of suffering. But in truth, no-thing will ever make us happy. Happiness ensues directly and continuously from the way we live our lives.

For example, I (Targ) cowrote an earlier book, *Miracles of Mind,* describing the best data from psychical research, including my own work at Stanford Research Institute. I thought it was a wonderful book, but I simply could not find a publisher. I was very unhappy. Finally, I met an editor who agreed with me about the book's potential and agreed to publish it. After signing the contract, I finally had several microseconds of uninterrupted happiness, before dropping back into a state of concern and worry about how the book would be advertised and what shows I would appear on to promote it. Now, a decade later, I have learned to enjoy the process of writing, hope the book will be helpful, and let the future of the book take care of itself. The change came as I internalized the teaching of Dzogchen Buddhism. My awareness became more spacious and autonomous. My sense of who I am is no longer determined by how many books I sell. And I let go of my publisher father's teaching that who you are is determined by your position on the *New York Times* bestseller list.

Our goal is to encourage you to overcome the conditioning of two-value logic in order to experience life with unprejudiced, nonconceptual, naked awareness, in which we give up judgment, naming, and grasping. It can't be said too often that *the map is not the territory*. In other words, our conditioned awareness is not reality. Because of our dualistic conditioning—our education, memories, and traumas—it is *we* who give all the meaning there is to everything we experience, rather than something outside ourselves that has *inherent* meaning. In other words, the flower does not give *us* meaning, *we* give meaning to the flower. Much of this conditioning stems from the structure of our language. So, if we become conscious of how the shortcomings of language limit our experience, we can begin to create new linguistic tools that recognize the differences of personal experiences and the generalizations that come from the way we use language. For example, at my (Targ's) laser laboratory at Lockheed, we had a powerful laser operating at 5,200 angstroms. There was no doubt as to its wavelength, but there were passionate disagreements among the engineers as to whether to call the laser's light green or blue. In fact, there is no fixed separation between green and blue, because they lie on a spectrum that is absolutely undivided from red to yellow to blue. We arbitrarily assign the words "blue" and "green" based on our conditioning, perception, and experience. As we change our awareness of language, we will change the way we experience everything. We do make agreements about language, but let's not pretend that agreed-upon language is immutably true.

Getting Out of Hell Free

Actually, you *can* escape from the conditioning of the Aristotelian mind trap, which is really ego-based, where your attention is fixed on who you think you are and what you think you are doing—accomplishments versus relationships. The only freedom is self-realization—ordinarily hidden, yet intuitive. Lasting freedom is attained by entirely changing your mind. Freedom, however, is a discontinuous process. You're free, or you're stuck. You can't have ultimate freedom until your last toe is entirely out of the quicksand or out of the prison. You change your mind by waking up to the fact that the socioeconomic and cultural milieu is just a story. This might even mean breaking the rules. We always have the capability of saying, "Freedom—I won't do it!" As the existentialists know, there is no such thing as a compulsion; you are always free to choose. You attain personal freedom when you finally internalize that you are free to choose. The phrase "getting out of hell free" is meant to encourage you to make a choice.

Heaven and hell do indeed exist. Heaven is the experience that you have when you are experiencing peace, joy, and love. And that experience is available to you at any moment. Just like heaven, hell is also always available as the experience of fear, judgment, and resentment. You get to choose, at each moment, where you would like to reside. If you have found a way to quiet your mind and observe your thought processes, you have a much better chance of making the choice for heaven when that problem person or thought comes by and says "boo!" At first you will notice the occasional flash of anger, and you will let it go, because it no longer serves you. Eventually, that flash won't even arise. Then you are free.

But don't get too spaced out; you still need to exist in the material world. Your metaphysics must be coherent with your physics whenever you intersect with physical reality. You must reconcile the experiences of naked awareness, which is free of judgment, naming, and grasping, with life's other experiences and memories. The laws of Einstein do not mean that you forget everything you learned about stairs and bowling balls. If you drop a bowling ball on your toe, it will break your toe every time, whatever you may think about the bowling ball. But opinions about bowling as an activity is quite valid. After all, we want to avoid madness and communicate with other people, so it is very important to retain a coherent and harmonious cognitive and experiential relationship with ordinary space-time reality and with those around us. Emptiness does not mean nihilism. There actually is a physical reality. But, of course, we give it all its meaning.

This is not to say that there is no objective reality, or objective morality, where you can make up anything you want. Situational ethics, or moral relativism, can mistakenly lead to the belief that there is no objective morality and no absolute ethical standard in the universe. In other words, whatever is good for me is fine, no matter what harm it causes you. That is not what we are talking about. As you become less and less attached to materiality and celebrate freedom, you become aware of the other side of the coin, which is the responsibility of all of us not to create suffering. Once you have chosen freely, you can never say "somebody made me do it." Above all, your actions are not self-serving, but devoted to the alleviation of suffering.

Here are five specific suggestions that can help you get out of hell free. Each of these is discussed more fully in chapter 10.

1. *Embrace oneness:* Remember that we are one in consciousness. Every time you create a separation (through judgment), you create suffering—usually for yourself.

2. *Practice daily self-reflection:* It is essential to find a way to quiet the ongoing mental chatter. We recommend some sort of

daily meditation. Meditation really works—that's why so many people do it.

3. *Practice compassion:* Compassion is critical because you will notice that as you expand your awareness, there is no peace for you until there is peace for everyone. That's why watching or reading the news causes so much pain.

4. *Participate in a sangha:* The *sangha* is your spiritual community that allows you to give and receive love while participating in your spiritual practice. For peace of mind, it is essential to find a sangha. The three jewels of Buddhism are the Buddha (the Teacher), the dharma (teachings), and the sangha (spiritual community).

5. *Reflect positive thinking:* Surrender all judgment of others and yourself. Throughout the day, stay in touch with your own flow of loving awareness, which is who you are. Be in love, and don't go to sleep with the television news.

Finally, if you can't remember these practices, just remember the Buddhist prescription: empty, empty, happy, happy.

Space and Time

We are finally breaking out of the ontological straitjacket created by our dualistic thinking. Now, we are beginning to realize that we live in space-time and not space alone. The work of the physicist Albert Einstein and the great German mathematician Hermann Minkowski in the early twentieth century showed empirically that we cannot split "space" from "'time"; otherwise, we create delusional cosmology. Minkowski realized that space and time are inseparable and that they can best be described as joint elements of a four-dimensional manifold, which we now call the four-dimensional space-time continuum. Their work gave rise to modern atomic physics, quantum mechanics, and nonlocality. We no longer view ourselves as solid bodies but as bodies composed of molecules, atoms, subatomic particles, and mostly empty space moving in space-time. We are not just a body or a mind, we are really more like a body-mind. Just as space cannot be separated from time, the body cannot be separated from the mind.

Many of the world's problems are caused by the belief that the material substance of the universe is most important. This belief has led to a fear and scarcity mentality in which, like the Buddhist metaphor of the hungry ghost with a huge belly and pencil-thin throat, we can never get enough. It's no wonder we are confused, when we see magazine ads for home furnishings telling us to buy their stuff to "show who we really are" or that we can demonstrate "extraordinary love" with a diamond ring from Cartier. Materialism is a problem because it creates a distortion of who we are. The fear and scarcity mentality creates competition, a "me versus them" concept.

Perception of the "me versus them" is the ego-centered self-absorption that blocks the flow of awareness by focusing on the illusion of scarcity, rather than on our loving nature. If you are focused on your own needs, you are not able to give and receive love, which is what gives meaning to life. Indeed, the ground of our being is the collective consciousness itself. Here, our behavior becomes critically important as we learn to form our reality from the living fabric of the consciousness of creation. Hence, as we move toward self-liberation, it becomes critically appropriate to understand events as manifestations of our choice and freedom.

James Traitz's book *Don't Stop Your Mind* describes the modern film *Groundhog Day* as an amazing Zen parable.¹ In the movie, the hero plays a journalist who is going to cover a Groundhog Day event. He goes through his day, then goes to sleep, but when he wakes up the next day, it is a repeat of the day before. After different dramas unfold and are reported, the journalist realizes that his days are all the same. The bizarre repetitions of the same events drive him crazy, and he tries to kill himself. Even if he kills himself, however, he still wakes up the next day and it starts over as before. Ultimately, what happens is that he accepts existence as eternity. He begins living each day in the way of excellence, trying to perfect his every action for the benefit of others, as well as himself. The movie ends up with the character waking up absolutely happy, popping out of bed, stopping the clock radio, getting dressed, knowing exactly where a certain child will fall out of a tree and being there to catch him; knowing where a certain bus will hit someone, and pushing the person out of harm's way. Awakened, the hero's character is finally released from the time loop because he starts to redefine himself and his interactions with others. He then chooses to make each day more excellent than the one before.

Before understanding our true nature, many of us meet day-to-day life accepting it at face value and not looking beyond, beneath, within, or above. Most of us are engrossed in workaday routine, minds stopped on what surrounds us. The experience of awakening that we're seeking allows us to be consciously aware of our surroundings, rather than unconsciously unaware. It leads away from the self-absorbed world of "me" as the center of the universe and toward spaciousness of mind, with its tremendous power to bring new purpose, healing, and light into this world.

The mind has so much latent capacity that it can potentially reflect every interconnection of the world, and we can learn to experience this. Beginning with the methods of forgiveness, affirmations, and meditation (described later), we can each take a great step forward in the process of self-renewal, reconnecting with a universe teeming with life and consciousness.

In September 2004, *Newsweek* devoted more than 20 pages to informing its readers about the importance of mind and body science in "The New Science of Mind and Body." Unfortunately, it concluded that the "soul" is a kind of pocket PC. It solemnly told us, "Modern neuroscience has shown that there is *no user* [emphasis added]. The soul is in fact [simply] the information processing activity of the brain." We know that this could not possibly be true because our soul or our nonlocal awareness fills all of space-time and allows us to experience that spaciousness directly.

Sir John Eccles, Nobel prize–winning biophysicist, believed that a higher world of the mind manipulates the brain when we try to recall a memory event, recapture a word or phrase, or express a series of creative thoughts.[2] In this process, the "subconscious" exercises a superior interpretative and controlling role in the world of neurobiological events. This may be observed by sensitive persons who sometimes perceive outside stimuli even before any physical brain processes have taken place. We all can experience precognitive ability that allows us to ascertain future events *before they happen*. Incidents of precognitive ability have been reported since antiquity—for example, the Oracle of Delphi, the biblical accounts of Jesus foretelling his future sufferings, and laboratory experiments throughout the world for the past century. Previously, conventional science ignored psi, or psychical research, because these experiments were not repeatable to order. All this changed in the 1970s and 1980s, however, with the increasing accuracy and reliability of parapsychological experiments from laboratories worldwide.

Currently, scientists from Stanford Research Institute, Princeton and Edinburgh Universities, as well as various Russian institutes (e.g., Pavlov Institute and Odessa State University) are looking more seriously at the abilities of the mind to retrieve useful information from a remote source (described in chapter 7). We study precognition because there is compelling data indicating that people occasionally have very clear dreams of events they then experience the next day. This common experience is at variance even with Einstein, who has us slowly moving through space and time at a rate of one second per second, simply uncovering the present moment. (If we're creeping along in a relativistic way, that is, at the velocity at which we usually move, then Einstein thought we could not know the future—but he was wrong.) This linear approach, called the block universe, would not allow for the precognition we see. Researchers in precognition say that we can move along faster than one second per second. This is not to say that parapsychology is a spiritual path, but the fact that our awareness has mobility in both space and time shows that we could not possibly be merely physical bodies. Who we are is nonlocal awareness residing for a time as a physical body. This is the inescapable conclusion of a century of quantum theory and parapsychological research.

The new sciences of quantum physics and nonlocality have shown the inadequacy of Einstein's concept of relativity, by which physicists have been oriented to think of the universe as four-dimensional, with time as an inescapable thing-like dimension. From a new scientific perspective, it is important to view the future or the past as really present and knowable. There is also the possibility of multiple futures—each having a certain probability and each sending us certain signals that our minds could interpret. When people experience the future through precognitive dreams, it is as if they see a vision of the future, wherein the future already exists. Such occurrences do not violate the fundamental laws of physics; rather, we must expand the paradigm of science to explain how precognitive experiences can take shortcuts through nonlocal space-time.

We are beginning to understand that time can be altered, either speeded up or slowed down. Einstein understood the relativity of time (his view is still in favor today) even though he did not believe we could know the future, for which modern scientists now have very good evidence. For example, time can also have different manifestations depending on the velocity of the object. Thus a global positioning satellite must be corrected for time dilation because time moves more slowly for the satellite relative to the Earth (in general relativity, time dilation is calculated by integrating its space-time interval over its space-time path in any inertial frame). This brings to mind the famous twin paradox, a thought experiment in special relativity: Twin brothers decide that one of them will stay on earth, while the other takes a space journey on a rocket traveling at almost the speed of light. When the traveling twin finally returns to earth, it is observed that he is much younger than his earthbound twin (giving rise to the widely held belief that traveling keeps you young). This is an experimentally verified phenomenon called "time dilation."

But time is not what your conditioning may lead you to believe. Thus, to end our suffering we need to change our beliefs, which are based on a restricted perception of space-time and a restricted worldview. What do we mean by a restricted worldview? In the twentieth century, great breakthroughs took place in scientific thinking. Many scientists now admit that we must cast aside the old idea of *determinism,* that each stage of coming into being is completely controlled by what has already come into being. That is, science has begun to conclude that *conscious choice* can rule over chance or determinism.

Another change has occurred in the rejection of matter as the basis of physical reality, a notion that has been held sacrosanct since the publication of Newton's *Principia* in 1687. The view that matter is the basis of life is now seen by many as an illusion. A third change has occurred in our perception of time, not simply in changing our linear concept, but in confirming it as an arbitrary construct. Although time's very existence has allowed us to accomplish and know things within our evolutionary phase of life, we have now proven Einstein's theory that relativistic time can be speeded up or slowed down.

In recognition of the profound wholeness of nature, another change in our thinking is beginning to occur: our ability to move beyond the limited opportunities of the dualistic thinking process of Aristotle, which, as already said, is the foundation of much of Western science and religion. This change allows for choice. It liberates us from the limitations of two-valued logic. Things that seem poles apart and seemingly opposite are actually complementary rather than antagonistic. In music, for example, without the experience of dissonance, we would not recognize harmony. Without our knowledge of chaos, we would not appreciate order. Like light and dark, these polar opposites are each manifestations of a single whole. We see ourselves as distinct from our conditioning and our story. But many now believe that it is *nonlocal awareness, rather than matter* that is the ground of all being (explained in chapter 6).

Notes

1. James Traitz, *Don't Stop Your Mind*, Cleveland, OH: Arete Press (2003).

2. Sir John Eccles, *Facing Reality: Philosophical Adventures by a Brain Scientist*, New York: Springer-Verlag, 1970.

4

Nagarjuna's Philosophy: Changing Your Mind and Choosing Peace

Nothing beyond yourself can make you fearful or loving, because nothing *is* beyond you.

—*A Course in Miracles*

The logic of Aristotle lies on a familiar one-dimensional line that extends from a point we call "x exists" to another point called "x doesn't exist," where x stands for anything from mental abstractions like ghosts, demons, or angels to any other entity in question. This is an example of duality, as we have explained. On the other hand, the thought system of Nagarjuna moves from this one-dimensional line to fill an entire plane. It includes not only the Aristotelian line, but also a line at right angles to it, which extends from a point called "x exists and x does not exist" to "x neither exists nor does not exist." It literally brings an entire new dimension to logical thought. This expansion of our thought system from one dimension to two dimensions requires a total reformulation of how we determine what is true for us.[1]

Thus the description we offer of Nagarjuna's way of being in the world—his path to transcend suffering—will be both logical and experiential. It is impossible to use exclusively two-valued logic to show the fullness of possibilities. We need a four-valued logic system to describe a nonconceptual system of thought that leads to awareness of timeless existence, spaciousness, and the Divine. Some may feel that our approach lacks rigor, but we are confident that transformation of consciousness cannot be accomplished *solely* with an Aristotelian truth table. This is not an apology, just a description of the way things are.

We are encouraging you the reader to expand your awareness by thinking in entirely new, and frequently uncomfortable, ways. We know that for many, a day without judgment is like a day without sunshine. But this new way is a *nonconceptual and nondual path* that requires the relinquishment of judgment. Surrendering judgment does not mean, however, that we give up our ability to separate reality from illusion. Although we can't prove or guarantee that this path will eliminate your particular suffering, we are offering it here because we are confident that it will provide tools that can at least diminish suffering.

Western Aristotelian style philosophers have established a limited, binary logic that they expect us to apply indiscriminately to the world and our lives using conceptual and propositional forms (e.g., "Those who are not with us are with the terrorists").

Nagarjuna goes one step further. His nonconceptual dialectic or tetralectic of four points or "lemmas" goes beyond the black-and-white structure (di-lemma) of life and polarities mentioned in the previous chapter.

How can we alleviate human suffering and, in turn, influence events around us? We can begin by redefining ourselves beyond dualistic thinking. For centuries, psychologists, sages, and philosophers have proposed different methods for doing this. One of the most powerful attempts comes from a school of Buddhist thought called the Madhyamika (the Middle Way). Although an ancient philosophy, it is still valid today, teaching us how to begin dissolving the roadblocks we create for ourselves when we think "within the box," or when we parrot the echoes inherited from a "me versus them" worldview. Buddhist scholar Thomas McFarlane writes, "The Madhyamika philosophy was conceived in compassion, for its fundamental purpose is to liberate individuals from ignorance and suffering."[2] This philosophy wants to free us from the prison of a reified conventional truth, including scientific truth.

We do not expect the reader to necessarily embrace the whole Madhyamika philosophical program. But our experience is that internalizing, or even understanding, Nagarjuna's form of logic is, *all by itself,* a mind-expanding and mind-freeing path to spaciousness.

Using the Madhyamika method, we are instructed to deactivate—unplug—the fundamental concepts of Aristotelian thought. For the Aristotelian thinker, the more firmly you draw lines around things and between things, the more logical your mind becomes, the more exact is your science, and the more accurate is your view of reality. We are arguing here that all of life's experiences cannot be reduced to Venn diagrams (intersecting circles). Because two-valued logic compartmentalizes and isolates us and everything else, it frustrates any motion or impulse toward empathy and compassion.

In the early 1970s, the West became keenly interested in Buddhist texts, particularly in the Sanskrit, Tibetan, and Chinese schools of philosophy that lead to a higher awareness of nondualistic thinking. At the pinnacle of all these schools of reflective philosophy and psychology stands the work of the great genius of Buddhist thinking, the dharma master Nagarjuna. Although details of Nagarjuna's life are unclear, it appears that he was born a Hindu in India, sometime between 150 and 200 A.D., and later converted to Buddhism.

This brilliant South Indian thinker and writer brought a new critical perspective to Buddhist philosophy. In his commentaries on the Prajnaparamita Sutras—the Mahayana teachings on emptiness and the Perfection of Wisdom—Nagarjuna greatly clarified the difficult nondual aspect of the Buddha's teachings. For example, when the Buddha was asked, "Will these teachings be heard a hundred years from now?" he answered, "These are neither teachings nor not teachings." One might well be puzzled the first time such a statement is encountered in the Diamond Sutra, because it looks like a contradiction. Yet this answer is not a contradiction, but an invitation to experience a liberation!

Nagarjuna's commentaries on the Prajnaparamita ("Perfection of Wisdom") are considered the root texts of Madhyamika. They represent a philosophical and logical expansion of the teachings on emptiness (sunyata) or naked awareness free of conditioning. His teaching brings into question every idea that we humans have about the nature of reality. This has led some critics, peeking through the lens of dualistic two-valued logic, to view Madhyamika's system of logical argumentation as nihilism,

Nagarjuna: Often called "The Second Buddha," who has control over the sea sprites *(nagas)*

the delusion that everything including the self does not exist. We contend it is not nihilism (the complete denial of reality) but a method to overcome the confines of the so-called rational mind, wherein we can discover the true meaning of the Madhyamika and find *prajna* (wisdom) along with the most intimate and overlooked aspect of humanity—the power of consciousness.

In an interview in *What Is Enlightenment?* magazine, the Dalai Lama singled out Nagarjuna as one of the truly enlightened people of all time. Nagarjuna founded the Madhyamika or "Middle Way" school of Mahayana Buddhism in the second century A.D. What he created was a nonconceptual and nondual, or nonpolar, path *between* reductionistic materiality and nihilism. Materiality and nihilism can be seen as Aristotelian views of a single truth. The materialist says that the person is simply the sum of its parts, while the nihilist says that the person is an illusion. Nagarjuna said there is no single truth and introduced an open-ended philosophy which overcomes the shortcomings of Aristotelian dualism in which a thing is either true or not true.

According to Madhyamika, the root of all suffering lies in mistakenly separating ourselves from our own spacious nature, where space-time and body-mind are inseparable. Nagarjuna taught that concepts of division (especially those arising in dualistic logic) are false and they distort the true nature of reality; in fact, we must not grasp on to any ideas at all. When false notions like self-nature, the soul, or permanency are cleared away or "blown out" *(nirvana),* one sees with intuitive wisdom the true nature of things, as described in the Perfect Wisdom Heart Sutra (contained in the Prajnaparamita Sutras).

From Jonah Winters's clear and comprehensive thesis, we learn that Nagarjuna taught that ultimate reality is devoid of all dualities and thus is wholly impervious to conceptual thinking. It can only be accessed in nondual intuition, *prajna.*[3]

Through his philosophy, Nagarjuna worked to free the world from the errors of conditioned awareness, to save us from the suffering caused by the spell of concretized conventional truth, including reified scientific truth. How does he do this? Nagarjuna gives us tools and insights as he leads us step-by-step through the drama of our lives, through a maze of reality.

Rational Madness to the Rescue

The Madhyamika system of Buddhist philosophy is extremely sophisticated in its metaphysical implications. In fact, Nagarjuna's Madhyamika is revolutionary, for the practitioner must question the validity of knowledge as a whole.[1] So far-reaching are its implications that the three major schools of philosophy in India (Vaibhasikas, Sautrantikas, and Yogacarins) take the majority of Nagarjuna's logical statements as true. Nagarjuna introduced a four-logic system, or *tetralemma*, in which statements about the world can be: (1) true, (2) not true, (3) both true and not true, and (4) neither true nor not true (which Nagarjuna believed was the usual case). This is how we are able to be both a self and not a self; both separated as bodies and not separated in consciousness.

In the process of Madhyamika, any thinker can reach a level of higher logic that is "open-ended." Here, one moves from a binary logic of *excluded middle,* where things are either "yes" or "no," to a quaternary (fourfold) logic, including the middle and the ends surrounding it (yes, no, yes and no, neither yes nor no). The Nagarjunian logic is of unlimited wholeness, which also contains the empty set. When it negates itself, it leaves itself unnegated. It negates being, or sameness; it negates nonbeing, or difference; it negates both being and nonbeing as mixture and as fusion. For those who believe suffering is a "yes" or a "no" or even a "synthesis of the two," Madhyamika Buddhism uncovers the unity of suffering and nonsuffering behind the play of life in order to alleviate suffering in each act. We are shown how to go beyond words to become creator and liberator at the same time.

First, however, there must be a substantial change in what we identify as three-dimensional space and time, as well as an understanding of how the mind thinks in past, present, and future. Using Nagarjuna's method of reflection, the practitioner changes his or her thought processes, whereby the very act of thinking—the very understanding of the reality of life, the Real—is brought into a new and open-ended process of thought.

Yet what appears at first glance to be too abstract has a most wonderful use. With it, we can see that physics may well find its resolution of the so-called wave-particle paradox in a four-logic analysis. It is well known that, under the conditions of various experimental arrangements, light displays either wavelike or particlelike properties. What then, is the essential nature of light? This question may not be amenable to our familiar Aristotelian system of logic and may be better addressed by an expanded logic system. We might say, for example, that light is: (1) a wave, (2) not a wave, (3) both a wave and not a wave, or most correctly (4) neither a wave nor not a wave—because it can manifest as either (but never as both wave and particle) depending on the instruments used to make the measurement.

The two-valued Aristotelian logic we use every day is simply inadequate to describe the pluralistic data of modern physics, while the four-logic system of Nagarjuna is more appropriate.

Similarly, we have the famous teaching, "Do nothing, and let nothing be left undone," from the *Tao Te Ching*, written in China by Lao Tsu at the time of the Buddha. This is an instruction from emptiness (*sunyata*), indicating that inaction does not exclude effectiveness. Doing nothing is often the appropriate response. We call this seemingly paradoxical approach "rational madness" because it is an ordered logical form that transcends Aristotle. It is Nagarjuna's third lemma—both doing and not doing. Finding yourself caught on the horns of a dilemma implies a two-valued mind trap, and the solution generally lies "outside the box." By going beyond limited logic that forces false dichotomies, the mind is free to experience spaciousness and compassion.

The Tetralemma: The Logical Form of the Madhyamika

We would like to further clarify Nagarjuna's tetralemma. Noted Buddhist scholar Edward Conze presents the four lemmas as: "(1) x exists, (2) x does not exist, (3) x both exists and does not exist, and (4) x neither exists nor does not exist."[5] The modern Buddhist philosopher T. R. V. Murti characterizes it thusly: "These four alternatives represent all the possible standpoints from which every problem can be viewed; they also provide a schema under which all systems of philosophy can be classified."[6] Another way of looking at this is provided by Richard Robinson, a contemporary translator of Eastern texts, who views each lemma as representing an "existential quantification," each differing in the quantity of its constituent terms, so that: (1) All x is A, (2) no x is A, (3) some x is A and some is not A, and (4) no x is A and no x is not A.[7]

The Aristotelian logic of the excluded middle still exists in the first two Nagarjunian lemmas. It is present by virtue of the polarities "x" and "not x" on two consecutive points, namely "x" on lemma 1 and "not x" on lemma 2. Here, in a simple two-step structure of alternating opposition (x and not x), the thinker must cross an empty (excluded) middle ground in which he or she may never stop under penalty of destroying the procedure of the logic of the excluded middle. Such is the mental template of the boundary of the mind, in which there are two full terminal bounds and one "empty" middle bound that determines the so-called "duple law of negation." This duple law of negation is the basic syntactic mechanism of Aristotelian formal logic. Either you believe or do not believe something is real. The thinker is told to see his or her beliefs as anchored in one *or* the other. There is no room for a synergistic thinker who sees the many different experiences as complementary and nondual.

This duple and sequential schedule comprises the first two lemmas and effectively sets out the basic structure of choice that is the nerve of Western logic:

Either x (lemma 1)
Or not x (lemma 2)

For example, Federal Reserve chairman Alan Greenspan tries to prevent both inflation and recession by using one simple tool—the increase or decrease of interest rates. This is an example of Aristotelian two-valued thinking. The logical schedule comprising the two stacked lemmas says, in effect: Presented for your mind is an "x" at lemma 1; if you choose to hold at lemma 1 without moving on to a further posit, you may hold at lemma 1. But if you will move on, then presented for your aim is a hold-point of the mind at lemma 2. In moving on into the opposite or "negative point" (lemma 2), however, you must relinquish your assertional hold of the preceding point.

When the "thinker" goes beyond the first and second lemma, he or she transcends the logic of duality as a whole. In making the basic negation of lemma 3, one moves thought into a new post-Aristotelian logic with a different internal structure of decision and negation in it. The lemma 1 and lemma 2 negation is internal to the dualist system, but for the discriminating mind, we must also understand something more than the basic negation:

We must comprehend the system transcending negation. This means:

Both (x and not x), lemma 3
Neither (x nor not x), lemma 4

Thus the first step in going beyond Aristotelian logic is to lay down a new form of logic, the logic of the third lemma. This logic is reached by the basic negation of the second and first lemmas. The third lemma creates a new view of objectivity where the logic lies between eternalism and vacuity. By this rule of basic inversion (x and not x), we constitute a new logical base of conceptualization derived by complete negation of the preceding lemmas taken separately. Here the tetralemma is a logical form, where a dialectic is obtained both between the first and second lemmas and within the third and fourth lemmas. We also cannot reach the fourth lemma until we reflect and pass through the third lemma, but it takes great boldness of thought.

The logic of Nagarjuna's fourth lemma, however, goes beyond the logic of even many mainstream Buddhist traditions. It negates the logic of all the lemmas or logical relationships that have preceded it. Entirely open and unbounded, the fourth lemma ensures a way out of a problem by dissolving the boundaries and restrictive "scripting" for a person restricted by dualism. The fourth lemma is neither affirmation nor negation. It represents complementarity and the nonconceptual aspects of the world. You are neither a body nor not a body. We assume you are feeling more free and spacious already.

What does this mean for modern thought? The fundamental idea of our familiar Western logic is the Law of the Excluded Middle. No possible extension of an Aristotelian system can ever bring you logically to the spaciousness of Nagarjuna. A systematic *practice* of the tetralemma principles changes the awareness of the mind to allow a new understanding of reality. It requires the practitioner to exchange her or his own limited viewpoint, allowing the mind to transcend its own grip on reality and thought. The final success allows for the transcendence of this reality and the achievement of a state of liberation where all the sufferings that equate with the material plane become unreal. That this philosophical system is beyond the standard dialectical form and beyond a mere critique of reason is attested to by Murti:

> The Madhyamika dialectic tries to remove the conflict inherent in Reason by rejecting both the opposites taken singly or in combination. The Madhyamika is convinced that the conjunctive (x and not x) or disjunctive (neither x, nor not x) synthesis of the opposites is but another view. Rejection of all views is the rejection of the competence of reason to comprehend reality. *The real is transcendent to thought.*[8] [emphasis added]

The tetralemma, thus, is a formal system of assertions that exhausts the number of rational viewpoints taken regarding any existent reality, these viewpoints being held both at the personal level and at the level of a philosophical system. The tetralemma can also be seen, however, as a therapeutic tool, over and above its logical operations, in relieving the mind from suffering caused by thinking in only disjunctive white or black dualities. The tetralemma relieves suffering by giving us a synthesis as well as additional choices so we can recognize that we are neither our body nor our story.

Further, to overcome the fatal flaw of the two-valued illusion,

Nagarjuna understood that we cannot consciously place ourselves always in the position of the person who asserts: "No asser-
tion is perfectly true." According to Robinson, we should

> consider the tetralemma as an expedient device
> *(upaya)* that the Buddha [as awakened being] uses in giv-
> ing progressively higher instruction to the different
> grades of living beings. First the Buddha speaks of phe-
> nomena as if they were real . . . Next he teaches some
> hearers that phenomena are unreal . . . Thirdly, he
> teaches some hearers that phenomena are both real and
> unreal . . . To these who are practically free from passions
> and wrong views, he declares that phenomena are nei-
> ther real nor unreal.[9]

This could be what Ralph Waldo Emerson had in mind when
he wrote, "A foolish consistency is the hobgoblin of little minds."

Sunyata: Emptiness as Truth

The famous incompleteness theorem of Kurt Gödel is considered by many to be the greatest accomplishment of twentieth-
century mathematics. Gödel's discovery of incompleteness came
as part of his investigation of *Principia Mathematica,* written by
Bertrand Russell and Alfred North Whitehead as a defense of logi-
cism. (*Principia Mathematica* and Aristotle's *Organon* are the most
influential books on logic ever written.) Gödel showed that their
effort to reduce mathematics to a logical system of axioms was not
only incorrect, but also impossible! In strong agreement with
Nagarjuna, Gödel said that any suitably complex system of mathematics, or thought system in general, will have within it some ideas

or propositions whose *truth or falsity cannot be determined* within the system.[10] A well-known example of these problems occurs in Bertrand Russell's exploration of vicious circle paradoxes of the form "This sentence is false." If the sentence is true, it cannot state that it is false; if the sentence is false, isn't it also true? So the sentence cannot be either true or false and hence exemplifies a violation of the a priori requirements of cognition or Aristotelian logic. A similar well-known set theory conundrum asks, "Who shaves the barber who shaves everyone who does not shave himself?" Our slavish adherence to two-valued epistemology traps us in a closed, absolutist, and crazy-making mental paradigm.

A consequence of Gödel's incompleteness theorem is that in any suitably complex belief system, there will always be some questions that cannot be decided within the framework of the system, often establishing a paradox, rather than a contradiction. The introduction of Nagarjuna's four-logic, however, brings forth solutions to many paradoxes. Buddhist scholar Alan Wallace explains his Middle Way understanding of the mind-body duality situation. He writes in *Choosing Reality:*

> *Physical realism* asserts that physical entities exist independent of the mind, and *idealism* maintains that they are the same nature of the mind. The centrist view refutes both these positions by declaring that the very dichotomy between physical and mental phenomena has only a conventional existence.[11]

Likewise, Kurt Gödel understood that one had to step outside the system in order to construct new rules and new ways to express ideas, and even then one would probably never be able to consider the fullness of what is true. The Madhyamika system agrees with Gödel in this regard, because it introduces a reinterpretation of the reality of life and, as such, of the physical elements we call matter.

The Mahayana systems clearly recognize the need to speak of the denial of substance *(pudgala-nairatmya)* that paves the way to *sunyata,* which includes the negation of duality. According to Nagarjuna, *sunyata* is not nothingness, but it is Truth or the absoluteness of naked awareness, free of conditioning.[12] That is, emptiness or the denial of substance has to be understood as being devoid of a separate reality from the absolute, and as being of an impermanent nature. This equates to the Hebrew concept of the *Ain Soph,* which means "Limitless." But *Ain Soph* is derived from two words: *Ain,* which is "nothing" (or "not," which is similar to the concept of *sunyata*), and *Soph,* which means "end." It is when the two concepts come together that one arrives at the Limitless or the Infinite without boundaries and beyond logic. Nagarjuna's expertise was in handling the dialectics of "emptiness" (*sunyata*) versus substance and concepts. He offered his teaching as a unique instrument for overcoming every kind of system of dead-end thought that gives rise to suffering. Again Jonah Winters:

> Ultimate reality is devoid of all dualities and thus is wholly impervious to conceptual thinking. It can only be accessed in nondual intuition, *prajna.* There are thus two levels of truth: the everyday, relative truth and the higher, absolute truth. . . . If one wished to speak in absolute terms and seek the ultimate ground of being of the universe, one could say no more than that the universe is characterized by ultimate emptiness. This is not a pessimistic denial of existence, though, but rather just a

description of the way things are. One who sees the true nature of things simply perceives that they are empty of self-nature. This realization, far from being nihilistic, is actually the very means by which liberation is achieved.[13]

Thus Winters contends emptiness or *sunyata* is a description of the way things are—impermanent and without essences or self-nature. In contrast, Aristotelian logic represents the outward, objective extension of "things" and their analysis. It is this very premise of analysis that tells us to make divisions and limitations, define boundaries, and deny the contiguity of consciousness. Aristotelian logic is all about making distinctions. Buddha taught that every time you make a distinction, you make an error. For example, we believe that we are separate from others. We have separate cultures. We are limited by our own abilities. We are limited by the world we exist within. These divisions, which are inherent in our logical reasoning, bring us face to face with the importance of introducing *sunyata* into our minds. In the broadest terms of *sunyata,* our life system is constructed using the principles of the empirical phenomenal world, which is provisionally established as real and then shown ultimately to be not real. This means that what we see as our limitation or as separation is also not real. Our minds are limitless. Peace and spaciousness are always available.

Just as Aristotle provides the classic example of a purely intellectual analysis of reality and, by this very fact, introduces a walled perception of existence, Nagarjuna shows us that separation is only an illusion. At the same time, the concept of emptiness as truth leads Western logicians to accuse Nagarjuna of nihilism. Nagarjuna affirms, however, that all of reality is mutually dependent, a single entity. Th. Stcherbatsky further defines

this term as "One-without-a-second." At the same time, so important is the concept of emptiness to the Madhyamika that the
alternative name for the system as a whole is *Sunyavada*, the doctrine of emptiness or seeing with naked awareness. McFarlane
further defines the term:

> *Sunyata*, as emptiness, means that the conventional
> world is not, as we fancy it, composed of substances
> inherently existing; but rather these entities are devoid
> of inherent substance—they are empty. It is important to
> point out that what is denied by this statement is not the
> conditioned world itself, but our clinging to it as
> absolute, our ignorance.[14]

Some scholars, like Harsh Narain, afford a limited interpretation of the Madhyamika as a system of nihilism. Throughout
his article "Sunyavada: A Reinterpretation,"[15] he, like other critics of the system, makes use of the term *sunyata* in its literal sense
of "pure void," equating this "void" with absolute nonbeing (the
position of the second lemma). However, Stcherbatsky declares

> that the term *sunya* is in Mahayana a synonym of
> dependent existence *(pratitya-samutpada)* and means not
> something void, but something "devoid" of independent
> reality *(svabhava-sunya),* with the implication that noth-
> ing short of the whole possesses independent reality, and
> with the further implication that the whole forbids [as
> unreal] every formulation by concept or speech (*nispra-
> panca*), since they bifurcate *(vikalpa)* reality—and never
> directly sees it—this is attested to by an overwhelming
> mass of evidence in all the Mahayana literature.[16]

As a last word on nihilism versus the concrete and to refute criticisms of the Madhyamika (Middle Way), we think it fair to say that a majority of serious students of the system would agree with Murti when he says:

> It might be thought that the Madhyamika dialectic ends in utter negation and the system is a special pleading of elaborate nihilism. The criticism is misinformed and misses the nature of the system. The method is negative, and not the end. Denial of the competence of thought to cognitive reality is not denial of the real. Thought is not the only form of knowledge. The Madhyamika dialectic rises by three "moments" to an intuitive or non-dual knowledge of the real. There is first the clash of the views *(drsti-vada)* as indulged in by dogmatism. The second moment arises with awareness of these views or thought-constructs as a falsification of the real. This is enforced by *reductio ad absurdum* arguments. The utter negation of thought is at once the intuition of the *tattva* (Real) from the duality of "is" and "not-is." It is *prajna* (wisdom) or *jnanam advayam* [nondualistic truth], and is identical with the Absolute.[17]

Thus Nagarjuna was not preaching nihilism but defining *sunyata,* which is a metaphor for the Absolute (ultimate reality), as in what is called *paramartha* (the unconditional stage of life): The Real is nondual, that is to say, free from all empirical predicates and relations. It is *sunya,* devoid of every kind of determination. We naturally want to identify with our past or present experiences that define who we think we are, but if we experience difficulties or suffer losses, we are confronted with mental suffering. By moving into the knowledge of the Absolute, as well as the negation of what we perceive as real, the platform itself becomes "devoid" or removed and all the "players" that exist become merely part of the All, whereby we are able to release the thought-forms that have brought us to the state of suffering and sadness, realizing anew there is no true separation. Here we begin to affirm that "happiness" is a state of mind and we can transcend "suffering" by surrendering it to the "Absolute." At the same time, we also need, with humility, to drop our old emotional bindings that keep us from realizing this Truth, that is, to become "emptied" of our lower emotional attachments and our attachment to personal cherished outcomes.

The tetralemma is intended to teach us of the Buddha's *Dharmakaya*—how to transcend limited time and space. And how can we transcend time? In describing the Middle Way between absolutism and nihilism, we could agree with Nagarjuna that time is merely a dependent set of relations, not separate in its own right, and certainly not the inherently existent vessel of existence it might appear to be.

In conclusion, the fundamental teaching is that the world outside our physical body exists but is devoid of inherent meaning. There are things and events out there, but we give them all the meaning they have for us. Most of our suffering is due to the meaning that we reflexively assign to things we experience, because of our conditioning. This conditioning is the source of our suffering. We overcome the suffering by trading in our conditioned awareness for naked awareness and freeing ourselves from painful gut reactions to occurrences that are meaningless in themselves. Freedom is all about choosing. Four-logic teaches us that the tiger eating the gazelle is neither good nor bad; it is simply a tiger. The event is devoid of meaning; it requires an observer.

Four-logic takes the philosophical view of mutual coarising about both tigers and terrorists. Like the tiger in the savannah, the behavior of the terrorist who blows up a building was set from the seeds scattered in the mists of past centuries. In any case, terrorist activity is not an independent event but the manifestation of mutual coarising over centuries, from the Crusades to Lawrence of Arabia, or what some call planetary consciousness. We all share responsibility for this mutual coarising because of our conditional awareness and behavior. As Chögyam Trungpa teaches, unconditioned wisdom "is realizing that your own wisdom as a human being is not separate from the power of things as they are. They are both reflections of the unconditioned wisdom of the cosmic mirror. Therefore there is no fundamental separation between you and your world."[18] If you can manage to be actually present, you have the opportunity to make a choice about how you affect and experience the world.

Notes

1. The salient features for chapters 4 and 5 were inspired by an earlier paper on Nagarjuna's Madhyamika philosophy by J. J. Hurtak, entitled "Madhyamika Buddhism: An Example of the Violation of Language," written in 1970 for the Center for the Study of Democratic Institutions in Santa Barbara, California.

2. Thomas McFarlane, *Sacred Science: Essays on Mathematics, Physics, and Spiritual Philosophy*, 1995, available at: http://www.integral science.org/sacredscience/SS_title.html.

3. Jonah Winters, *Thinking in Buddhism: Nagarjuna's Middle Way*, dissertation for Reed College in Portland, Oregon, 1994, available at: http://bahai_library.com/personal/jw/other.pubs/.

4. Mysore Hiriyanna, *Outlines of Indian Philosophy*, London: George Allen & Unwin, 1964, p. 207. In looking at how the dualistic mind has a tendency to cling to mental conditions of "suffering" there is a need for sectional studies of how the Madhyamika works, observing the

priority of synchronic studies over diachronic studies and isolating classes of arguments as to why there is no single truth.

5. Edward Conze, *Buddhist Thought in India,* London: George Allen & Unwin, 1962, p. 219. I (Hurtak) have reversed the order in which Conze places the third and fourth lemma, since their original placement by him is an obvious error; all other interpreters agree that the conjunctive affirmation of the first two lemmas precedes their disjunction negation, and this is the form exhibited in the original texts. See also Conze, *Buddhism: Its Essence and Development,* New York: Harper & Brothers, 1959, p. 136.

6. T. R. V. Murti, *The Central Philosophy of Buddhism: A Study of the Madhyamika System,* London: George Allen & Unwin, 1955, p. xiii. The nuggets of this teaching known as the "the Central Philosophy of Buddhism" are available in translations of Chinese writings of Madhyamika Buddhism by the immediate disciples and colleagues of Kumaarajiiva, the great fifth-century A.D. translator of these ancient texts from the Indic language; the contemporary translator of oriental texts, Richard Robinson; and a handful of prized scholars including T. R. V. Murti and Edward Conze.

7. Richard H. Robinson, *Madhyamika Studies in Fifth-Century China,* University of London thesis, 1959.

8. Murti, *Central Philosophy,* p. 128.

9. Richard H. Robinson, *Early Madhyamika in India and China,* Madison: University of Wisconsin Press, 1967, p. 56.

10. Kurt Gödel, in Ernest Nagel and James R. Newman, "Gödel's proof," *Scientific American* 194:6 (June 1956).

11. B. Alan Wallace, *Choosing Reality: A Contemplative View of Physics and the Mind,* Boston: New Science Library, 1989.

12. Dr. Rewata Dhamma Ven, "Sunyata, Emptiness and Self-emptying, Kenosis," Buddhist-Christian Dialogue Conference, London: March 27, 1993.

13. Winters, *Thinking in Buddhism.*

14. McFarlane, *Sacred Science.*

15. Harsh Narain, "*Sunyaveda:* A reinterpretation," *Philosophy East and West* 12:4 (1964), pp. 311–338.

16. Th. Stcherbatsky, *The Central Conception of Buddhism and the Meaning of the Word "Dharma,"* Motilal Banarsidass, 1994, p. 41.

17. T. R. V. Murti, "Metaphysical Schools of Buddhism," in S. Rhadakrishnan, *History of Philosophy, Eastern and Western,* London: George Allen & Unwin, 1952, p. 207.

18. Chögyam Trungpa, *Shambhala: The Sacred Path of the Warrior,* Boston: Shambhala, 1988.

5

Nagarjuna and the Challenge of the Two Truths

It is not that people won't betray you. It is not that your heart won't break again and again. Opening to whatever is present can be a heartbreaking business. But, let the heart break, for your breaking heart only reveals a core of love unbroken.

—Gangaji, *The Diamond in Your Pocket*

Nagarjuna's purpose in emphasizing nondual emptiness *(sunyata)* is to bring our ordinary consciousness (which is conditioned) as close as possible to naked unconditioned consciousness. The goal is for us to come directly into contact with this naked awareness, which is who we are. Naked awareness is our entry point to the experience of nonconceptual emptiness that is free of *me* and *mine*. Suffering is instantaneously released when we finally surrender *me* and *mine;* suffering will not and cannot be released until that surrender is accomplished. The fundamental teaching is that the pristine spacious experience of naked awareness, or awakened Self *(bodhichitta),* must be free of the egoic *me.*

Nagarjuna demonstrates with almost mathematical precision that suffering is unnecessary if not impossible when we experience the true nature of reality. Suffering is the result of our limited understanding of the world as composed of separate, discrete entities that interact with each other and with our selves. Nagarjuna addressed this problem in the Two Truths doctrine, which is based on the view of two realities—*relative* or *subjective* reality and *ultimate* reality. Our understanding of the two truths is important to our happiness and freedom from suffering because it provides us the tools to distinguish reality from illusion. In our daily life, direct perception and experience of the world are hugely clouded by our projections and preconceptions, causing significant misapprehensions.

Relative or conventional reality involves our everyday experience of the world and is often based on culture and language. For example, Christians, Muslims, and Jews each have their own "true" way of worship. We agree to call a thing a table if it is composed of four posts and a plank and we use those parts in a certain way. *A Course in Miracles* (ACIM) expresses conventional reality by saying, "I have given everything I see all the meaning it has for me."

The Meaning of Schmutz

My (Targ's) parents, William and Anne, were, respectively, a distinguished publisher (*The Godfather, Andersonville,* and others) and a successful press agent. One night at a party at my parents' home in Chicago, my father's best friend and business partner spied a layer of dust on the windowsill behind some curtains. He took the opportunity to leave a little calling card by writing the Yiddish word *schmutz* (dirt) in the dust with his finger. After the party, my mother spotted this billet-doux and pointed it out to my father, who considered it an intolerable insult to my mother and him. As a result, his friend, whom I as a seven-year-old considered my jolly uncle Louis, was severed from all communication of any kind. Even decades later, when I became an adult, he and his name were still persona non grata in our house.

Another family, in another time, might have laughed and wiped up the dust, even perhaps put a "schmutz" card in Louis's napkin the next time he came for dinner. Nagarjuna would say that the insult cannot exist without a person to perceive it as an insult. We do not have to collect resentments and enemies and carry them around with us. Lack of forgiveness is as exhausting as it is unnecessary. Fortunately, freedom affords us the opportunity to choose again at any given moment. By freedom, we mean the ability to surrender our conditioning and our slavish defense of our ego. It's our conditioned awareness that renders us incapable of understanding the difference between relative reality and ultimate reality.

Ultimate reality or ultimate truth is nonconceptual and nondual, what the great twelfth-century Buddhist master Longchenpa calls the "basic space of phenomena" in his sublime book on that subject.[1] The ineffable nature of ultimate reality is expressed in the aphorism, "The Tao that can be spoken is not the true Tao." Your naked, *unconditioned* awareness—nondual intuition—gives you access to this basic space of phenomena.

Thus we speak of two aspects of reality or truth: relative and ultimate. Yet Nagarjuna taught that there are no fundamental differences between the two realities and that individual existence cannot be grounded outside the context of everyday experience. Therefore ultimate reality is based on relative reality, and *both realities are one and the same, not separate, not divisible, but dependently coarising.* The Vimalakirtinirdesa Sutra states, "To say *this* is conventional and *that* is ultimate is dualistic. To realize that there is no difference between the conventional and the ultimate is to enter the dharma door of nonduality." The division is only perceptual. It stems from the illusion of the ego-self defining what is "real" for *me*. This blocks our true ability to see and understand the ultimate reality, where the writing in the dust on the windowsill may have been a friendly gesture. Although all perceptions may be valid as a relative reality, sticking to one and not being willing to look at all other relative realities is the illusion that separates the relative from the ultimate. It's strange how a person's whole life can be reoriented by the way a few dust particles settle on the surface of reality.

Khenchen Thrangu Rinpoche writes similarly:

> Conventional truth concerning the way all appearances and experiences function, and the ultimate truth concerning the lack of objectifiable reality in everything, are inseparable; they are not two different things but rather an integrated whole. This is the basic viewpoint of Madhyamika, as expounded by Nagarjuna, and is the description of the actual viewpoint on reality of an enlightened Buddha.[2]

Everything Is Dependently Coarising

Nagarjuna taught the folly of attempting a dualistic explanation of ultimate reality by separating it from our conventional experience of the world. The empirical world is our "means" to the unconditional understanding of the ultimate. The noncon-ceptual truth beyond duality is the "end."[3] This suggests that we are to be consciously in the world and, at the same time, not be restricted by it. *In practical terms, when we give up seeing the world through the lens of our conditioning, we no longer project our fears, hopes, and prejudices onto everything we encounter.* The importance of the "two truths" teaching is to point this out. Then we can experience naked awareness, limitless mind, and unbounded consciousness. Nagarjuna's tetralemma helps us to make this shift by destroying the idea that things have an independent existence. Along this same line, the great physicist Werner Heisenberg taught that "The idea of an objective real world whose smallest parts exist objectively in the same sense that stones or trees exist, independently of whether or not we observe them . . . is impossible."[4]

The great eighth-century writer Shankara wrote in his *Crest-jewel of Discrimination*[5] that our most significant life goal is to dis-cern reality from illusion. Nagarjuna taught that when we cease reifying things and the self, we then drop our emotional attach-ments to objects, personas, and concepts of the world. We sur-render the ego by giving up the notion of "I" and "mine." Then we can experience the undifferentiated nature of ultimate real-ity. Until that point of realization, we misperceive existence. The illusion of separation inhibits our awareness of ultimate reality by confining our awareness to only a small part of reality. As Nagarjuna teaches, conventional reality and ultimate reality are not separate realities. He illuminates the truth of nonduality through his teachings on emptiness and dependent arising in which he says that all things, concepts, and persons are empty of self-nature and only arise to exist dependently on other factors. To be perfectly clear, the teaching here is that nothing at all exists independently. What we're describing here is not esoteric, but simply mental housecleaning. It should be done daily, or at least every spring.

A more thorough understanding of the two truths includes an understanding of the central theme of the *Madhyamika-karika*—emptiness or *sunyata,* as we discussed in chapter 4. Nagarjuna said that understanding emptiness leads to a greater truth of how things really are. Furthermore, he said that all things are empty and he used the tetralemma to prove it. Again, it is important to remember that emptiness does not deny the existence of conventional reality or things, but says that all things have no self-nature or intrinsic essence. Nothing exists on its own, divided or separated from other things. Everything is interdependent and cannot exist without other things, including the Self. For example, a location cannot exist without an object in that location, and an object cannot exist without a location. This is the meaning of emptiness and dependent arising. Einstein said the same thing in his general relativity theory: We cannot have empty space. The object and its mass define the space. Recent (relativistic frame-dragging) experiments with a gyroscope spinning in space investigate the gravitational effects of the spinning earth (NASA Gravity Probe B Mission). The experiments are expected to show that the nature of space itself is affected by the spinning earth, just as Einstein predicted. Nagarjuna explains:

Whatever is dependently coarisen
That is explained to be emptiness
That, being dependent designation
Is itself the middle way.
Something that is not dependently arisen,

Such a thing does not exist
Therefore a non-empty thing
Does not exist.[6]

Emptiness and dependent arising are inseparable. Nothing has independent existence and nothing can manifest on its own. Buddha further explicates dependent arising:

When this is present, that comes to be
From the arising of this, that arises
When this is absent, that does not come to be
On the cessation of this, that ceases.[7]

Since nothing can exist on its own and everything is dependent arising, reality cannot be two separate things. There is no correctness to the idea of "us" and "them."

In using Nagarjuna's tetralemma—the four lemmas—we begin to question our own reality through the Madhyamika system of reasoning. We gain a new vision beyond the illusion of a "single truth." Nagarjuna's teaching of the Two Truths—*conditioned truth* and *naked truth*—is important in understanding that any "single truth" is an illusion. The fourth lemma, in particular, introduces us to a transcendence of reason encompassing plural truths—the important idea that most things are neither this nor not this. We go beyond two-valued logic into an expanded awareness, which allows us to transcend limitations of our ordinary awareness of space-time existence. In the Madhyamika system, this transcendence or *prajna* is the wisdom identified with undifferentiated intuition and ultimate reality. As Gilbert and Sullivan said, "Things are seldom as they seem. Skim milk masquerades as cream." (*H.M.S. Pinafore*)

The intent of the doctrine of Two Truths is to move us beyond the phenomenal sphere of events and activities to new realms of being where we find the ultimate undifferentiated and unseparated from the locus of awareness. This is the state of *prajna*, wisdom that comes through an intuitive identification with ultimate reality (spaciousness). That is, the ontological status of *prajna* requires a mystical intuition of the ultimate that comes about once the logical reasoning of the first three lemmas has been exhausted. This entire movement is clear in Nagarjuna's *Madhyamika-Sastra* 2:XVII:

What is the Buddha after his Nirvana?
Does he exist or does he not exist,
Or both, or neither?
We will never conceive it.[8]

Murti tells us: "The death of thought is the birth of wisdom; devoid of distinction [judgment], it leads to wisdom."[9] The death of thought means the death of Aristotelian dualistic thought, the limited logic of the perceiver and the perceived. Such thoughts or concepts create distinction or separation. Perfect wisdom allows release from the naming and grasping that create separation and suffering. Again, the four lemmas help us break out of this dualistic thinking.

In a soul-searching sketch, then, the system may be quickly, however grossly, summed up in this manner: The individual finds himself in a phenomenal world of unhappiness, in which the Buddha tells us in the first of his Four Noble Truths, "To exist is to suffer." It is as if he is saying: This phenomenal realm *(samsara)* is composed of subject-object relationships. This is further explained by the second Noble Truth: "Suffering is caused by attachment, craving, or desire." This obviously expresses a subject-object bifurcation—separation and judgment—as the root cause of suffering. As with the four lemmas, we must understand the first two Noble Truths to appreciate the last two of the Noble Truths. We must learn about the possibility of choices (lemmas 1 and 2). In the same way, we must develop and experience a sense of self in order to discover that the concept of self is an illusion. The third and fourth Noble Truths are: "The end of suffering is attainable" and "the Eightfold Path leads directly to the end of suffering." The Eightfold Path is generally associated with: Right View, Right Intention, Right Speech, Right Action, Right Livelihood, Right Effort, Right Mindfulness, and Right Concentration.[10] Adhering to the elements of the Eightfold Path keeps us on a trajectory of freedom and spaciousness. Departing from the path does not mean we are bad, but it deflects our attention from the direction we want to be headed. More is said about the Eightfold Path in the notes to this chapter.

Schrödinger's Cat

Murti further states that although unconditioned awareness transcends thought, it is certainly accessible to us in intuition. Intuition is inherently nondual. Our intuition is our mind's access to nonduality and especially to lemma 4: A thing is neither true nor not true. For example, in modern quantum physics, we know that there is no separation between the observer and the observed. A famous puzzle in modern physics is the "Schrödinger cat paradox," in which at the conclusion of an experiment, the poor cat is both alive and dead! The great Austrian physicist Erwin Schrödinger proposed this thought experiment to illustrate one of the conceptual problems in quantum mechanics. This problem is called the measurement principle of indeterminacy, which says that a quantum state is undetermined until it is measured or observed. The following is Schrödinger's description of his experiment.

> One can even set up quite ridiculous cases. A cat is penned up in a steel chamber, along with the following diabolical device (which must be secured against direct interference by the cat): in a Geiger counter there is a tiny bit of radioactive substance, so small that perhaps in the course of one hour one of the atoms decays, but also, with equal probability, perhaps none; if it happens, the counter tube discharges and through a relay releases a hammer which shatters a small flask of hydrocyanic acid. If one has left this entire system to itself for an hour, one would say that the cat still lives if meanwhile no atom has decayed. The first atomic decay would have poisoned it. The Psi function [wave equation] for the entire system would express this by having in it the living and the dead cat (pardon the expression) mixed or smeared out in equal parts.
>
> It is typical of these cases that an indeterminacy originally restricted to the atomic domain becomes transformed into macroscopic indeterminacy, which can then be resolved by direct observation. That prevents us from so naively accepting as valid a "blurred model" for representing reality. In itself it would not embody anything unclear or contradictory. There is a difference between a shaky or out-of-focus photograph and a snapshot of clouds and fog banks.[11]

Basically, Schrödinger is saying that because of the way the experiment is set up, the cat has a 50 percent chance of being alive and a 50 percent chance of being dead. It is just as likely that the cat is alive as that it is dead, so Schrödinger said that until the box is opened, the cat is both alive and dead. This is obviously false. The cat cannot be both alive and dead at the same time, but it illustrates the limits of Aristotelian logic. Just as in the case of wave-particle duality, we would say here that the unobserved cat is "neither alive nor not alive." This state of affairs, where the cat is neither alive nor not alive at the same time, is the real meaning of the *superposition of states* in the quantum mechanical wave function. (Physicists describe everything in the world in terms of wave functions comprising a thing's momentum and position in probability space.)

The principle of superposition is analogous to Nagarjuna's identification of dependent arising, without which nothing can be said to exist in any identifiable way. The final observation of the cat is what precipitates the collapse of the quantum mechanical wave function by revealing the feline's final state. So the unobserved cat exemplifies the fourth lemma where the cat is neither alive nor not alive. As soon as we open the box and observe the cat, the wave function is collapsed, superposition is resolved, and the cat is reified in one of those two states, dead or alive. The principle of superposition claims that while we cannot determine what the state of any object is, it is actually in all possible states simultaneously, as long as we do not look. It is the measurement that causes the object to be limited to a single possibility. Thus superposition is not only a problem in quantum mechanics, it is also another example of the limits of Aristotelian two-valued logic.

Intuition and Logic

The principle of superposition and the transcendence of Aristotelian thought allow our conscious mind to be more intu-

itive, unrestricted, and unconditioned. The real test of this philosophy, however, is in applying Nagarjuna's four lemmas to our
everyday lives and the here and now. The following are practical
steps for developing intuitive wisdom. They are: (1) the dissolving and surrender of egotism and dogmatism, (2) the applica-
tion of self-criticism and naked awareness, and (3) the
incorporation of new nondual logical forms. This transformation requires honesty, fearlessness, and practice. For example,
the interrelation of the physical and non-physical world often
manifests in the state of our health. My body is made of atoms,
molecules, and physical systems. If I am ill, some part must need
repair. What actually might be causing the illness is my response
to an angry partner, a crazy boss, or even a wayward thought. So
we have a physical illness in response to a nonphysical event.
And we now know that sustained stress of any kind can not only
make you sick, but also make you stupid (by directing blood
away from the cognitive centers to your muscles and the reptil-
ian brain). So our bodies control our minds just as our minds
control our bodies. Body and mind are mutually coarising.

Nagarjuna's logic system attempts to show us a way to transcend dualistic thought patterns through the realm of rational
discourse. We are again presenting the four lemmas as an illus-
tration of his methods. We must first negate the first two lemmas: (1) this is true and (2) this is not true. The third lemma is
the attribution of two contradictory qualities: (3) this is both
true and not true. And the fourth lemma is a denial of two contradictory qualities: (4) this is neither true nor not true. Lemmas
3 and 4 describe the Middle Way, dissolving polarities and artificial separations. It's as though all beings have a fundamentally
complex nature. In mathematics, we would say we have both *real*
and *imaginary* parts, corresponding to a real, concrete material

part, in addition to an imaginary, spiritual, dependently coarising part.

To think in the negation of logical thought can be baffling if one has had little or no introduction to the Madhyamika system. Something or someone you thought about as real, you must also place into a new relationship and consequently consider unreal. But it is not unreal as if it never existed; it is unreal in that it has no independent existence. An entity is neither being nor nonbeing. It is "being" only in relation to something else. Until dependent arising, the entity is "nonbeing" or empty of individual essence. As we read in Nagarjuna's *Madhyamikakarika* XXIV:9: "There is no entity that is not dependent. An absolutely non-relational entity does not therefore exist."

The Madhyamika thinkers, while using all the resources of dialectic philosophy and logical disputation, search to arrive at an approximate idea of the unconditioned understanding of ultimate reality. But this understanding remains beyond the comprehension of those who look for release from pain and suffering outside themselves in ritualistic or psychological saviors. Release comes from within through change in our perception of what is real and not real, and through seeing our relationship to the whole. When we view the world and people as an interrelated whole, we lose the "I" versus "they" thought construction that creates competition and separation. This reality is only accessible to one who sees beyond the duality and illusion of separation.

The Model of the Real and Unreal

Everything real is interdependent and nothing unreal exists. The fundamental cause of suffering has traditionally and correctly been identified with ignorance of our true nature. Ignorance is the illusion of separation between subject and object, between self and other. This dualism is unreal in the sense that it creates divisions within ultimate reality. When we desperately attempt to maintain ego—individuality and autonomy—we maintain the belief that we are a body separate from other bodies. We continually seek ways to verify our own story, or self-identity. This is the insidiousness of the ego thought system. This illusory perception of ourselves *versus* others is the root cause of suffering from fears, anger, problematic relationships, addictive behaviors, and depression. Because of this mistaken identification of ourselves in relation to others, or in relation to the ultimate, we can spend an entire lifetime on futile obsessions, only creating further suffering. Seeing the dependent coarising nature of everything around us is the first step toward understanding the real nature of our experience.

Contrary to many Americans' cherished view of *rugged individualism,* Nagarjuna would agree with the idea that within a social fabric, "no man is an island unto himself." Everything real is interdependent. Nagarjuna taught that even our own existence "is not a thing in itself; it is what it is in relation to other entities, and these in turn depend on others."[12] This is the meaning of dependent arising and emptiness. Nagarjuna is establishing that all phenomena depend on each other, and any particular phenomenon lacks reality in any independent sense. The usual Western philosophical criterion for any phenomenon or entity to be ultimately real is that it possess its own being or essence, which means that it is "independent of conditions"—usually unrelated to others, ungenerated, everenduring. In the logic of Nagarjuna, if a thing must have independent existence in order to exist, then nothing exists because nothing has independent existence. Since the

Madhyamika sutras show that *there is no entity that is not in a relation* of mutual dependence, then there are none that possess own-being or self-nature. "If entities are relative, they have no real existence" (apart from the meaning that we give them), according to *Madhyamika-Sastra,* 1:X:1–2. Madhyamika thinkers do not deny our uniqueness, nor do they assert that beings have an independent or separate existence in any sense. Fire is not separate from the fuel for the flame, yet fire and fuel are unique.[13]

The Madhyamika system teaches us that there is no real difference between ultimate reality and the empirical phenomenal world including its noumenal or mind constructs. Differentiation is imposed by ignorance. When we realize that all phenomena, boundaries, and separations are illusions of our own making, then the idea of a separate ego maintaining a suffering state can be equally seen as an illusion. The world of illusion can be compared to a mirage; it is not absolute nonexistence, but it is a deception and greatly misperceived. An illusion appears to be real, and it is a tangible or visible phenomenon. The deception lies in its being mistaken for what it is not.[14] Behind all of these illusions, there is only undifferentiated identification with the ultimate. In the words of Nagarjuna in his *Madhyamika-Sastra* 2:XIX–XX:

XIX. There is no difference at all
Between nirvana and samsara.
There is no difference at all
Between samsara and nirvana.

XX. What makes the limit of nirvana
Is also the limit of samsara.
Between the two we cannot find
The slightest shade of difference.

The reason there is no difference between the bliss of nirvana and the ever-circling chaos of *samsara* is that they are both only ideas residing in consciousness. We, of course, always have the freedom to change our mind if we don't like what we are experiencing. In the preceding verse, Nagarjuna is addressing the Buddhist paradox or double bind that says "grasping for nirvana is still grasping!" As Alan Watts writes in *The Way of Zen,* "How can I let go of grasping, when trying is precisely not letting go. Trying not to grasp is the same as grasping." Watts then points out that "Nagarjuna answers, that all grasping, even for nirvana, is futile—for there is nothing to be grasped."[15]

The Madhyamika writers and teachers have constructed a system full of methodological triggers to bring one to intuitional realization. The tetralemma, which exhausts the possibilities of rationality, is designed to lead us into an intuition of the unity of all things. This is *prajna* (wisdom), which is beyond thought and word. It is obtained when we realize intuitively our identity with the ultimate. Murti confirms this by saying: "Nondual knowledge or wisdom is contentless intuition. Nothing stands out against it as an 'other' confronting it."[16] It's your nonlocal awareness filling all of space-time. The multidimensional hologram of nondual reality is undifferentiable.

The important concept of dependent arising or co-origination *(pratitya-samutpada)* in its ontological operation shows that there is nothing that cannot be placed in dependent relation with another thing or idea, when dependent relations are *all that is.* The fact that the world arises holographically rather than through simple causality is why our intuition allows us to know more than what our five senses provide. With this nonlinear understanding of mutual coarising, we can change the thoughts of suffering and division into the joy of awakened mind and the unity of Oneness. In the words of Nagarjuna's *Madhyamika-Sastra:*

The Perfect Buddha
The foremost of all Teachers I salute.
He has proclaimed
The Principle of (Universal) Relativity,
'Tis like blissful (Nirvana),
Quiescence of Plurality.[17]

Bending the Swords of Suffering

In the Aristotelian worldview, humans define themselves in terms of differences from one another. Wars and terrorism give ample evidence that humanity will gladly sacrifice every material thing, cause suffering to others, and even sacrifice their lives in the name of their convictions. In contrast, nondualism has the capacity to change perception through the reasoning of the four lemmas. As Nagarjunian thinkers, we understand the completeness and holism of humanity, including the "middle way," by transcending the perception of the one to the perception of the whole. Ultimately, this brings us to the consciousness of oneness, naked awareness, and self-liberation.

As a Mahayana master, Nagarjuna did not limit his teachings to the nature of the two truths and *sunyata*. He emphasized that, while living in this empirical reality, one must practice compassion in thought, speech, and action. "I am here only to be truly helpful" is taught throughout *A Course in Miracles*.[18] This is the middle way, the bodhisattva path, the way of emptiness and compassion.

Nagarjuna's mission was to show us how to free ourselves from the errors of conditioned awareness and from the suffering caused by the spell of reified or concretized conventional truth. His Middle Path of unconditioned naked awareness avoids the pitfalls of dogmatic absolutism on the right and mindless nihilism on the left. Slavery, war, crusades, or genocide would be impossible under such a system. Moreover, peaceful reconciliation within oneself leads to compassion and justice for others who are suffering. Such experiences help us break through to a new dimension of wisdom and understanding. Enlightenment is pure awareness, where the essence of the universe is consciousness itself.

With endless patience, Nagarjuna makes the point that fixed structuralism will destroy the very meaning of transformative action. When we negate the base of Aristotelian logic, we can use the logic of Nagarjuna. This thought system can overcome the narrow constructs of thinking that force the mind into *this* reality versus *that* reality. The logic of Nagarjuna lies between the polarities created by the logic of duality. While the Middle Way constitutes a powerful awareness of oneness and transcendence

"Nothing happens next. This is it."

of objects and ideologies, it is not in itself "holy." It is *upaya,* or a skillful means—a teaching device eventually to be discarded. When we break through symbols, myths, and religious stories that point beyond themselves to their transcendent reality, we discover the common source of unity.

In the victory over duality, we experience the disappearance of the illusion of separation from the Divine. *The Divine is already here.* The love that we seek is already within us—it is the flow of loving awareness breaking through the material strata of life and expressing who we are!

Notes

1. Longchen Rabjam, *The Precious Treasury of the Basic Space of Phenomena,* Junction City, CA: Padma Publishing, 2001.

2. Khenchen Thrangu Rinpoche, *Open Door to Emptiness,* Vancouver, BC: Karme Thekchen Choling, 1997, p. 48.

3. T. R. V. Murti, *The Central Philosophy of Buddhism: A Study of the Madhyamika System,* London: George Allen & Unwin, 1955, p. 253.

4. Werner Heisenberg, *Physics and Philosophy,* New York: Harper and Row, 1958.

5. Swami Prabhavananda and Christopher Isherwood (trans.), *Shankara's Crest-jewel of Discrimination,* Hollywood, CA: Vedanta Press, 1978.

6. Jay L. Garfield (trans.), *Fundamental Wisdom of the Middle Way: Nagarjuna's Mulamadhyamakakarika* by Nagarjuna, chapter 24: 18–19, New York: Oxford University Press, 1995, p. 69.

7. Bhikkhu Bodhi (trans.), *The Connected Discourses of the Buddha: A New Translation of the Samyutta Nikaya,* Boston: Wisdom Publications, 2000, p. 575 [part of the second watch of the night].

8. Murti, *Central Philosophy,* p. 140.

9. Murti, *Central Philosophy,* p. 128.

10. In Buddhist teachings, we find that suffering is principally caused by ignorance and craving. The ignorance of which they write is ignorance of who we are and our failure to separate reality from illu-

sion. The craving refers to our hope to find the solution to our dilemma outside ourselves, rather than inside. The Buddhist solution to this suffering is to follow the Noble Eightfold Path. Its goal is to free the individual from attachments and delusions.

The Eightfold Path comprises the following:

- Right View is the beginning and the end of the path; it simply means to see and to understand things as they really are and to realize the Four Noble Truths, especially impermanence.

- Right Intention can be described best as commitment to ethical and mental self-improvement and compassion.

- Right Speech means to tell the truth, to speak kindly and gently, and to talk only when necessary.

- Right Action means to act kindly and compassionately, to be honest, to respect the belongings of others, and to keep sexual relationships harmless to others.

- Right Livelihood means that one should earn one's living in a righteous way and that wealth should be gained legally and peacefully.

- Right Effort recognizes that mental energy can occur in either wholesome or unwholesome states. The same type of energy that fuels desire, envy, aggression, and violence can, on the other side, fuel self-discipline, honesty, benevolence, and kindness. Right effort is detailed to prevent the arising of unwholesome states.

- Right Mindfulness is the mental ability to see things as they are, with clear consciousness, not hooked by passions.

- Right Concentration for the purpose of the Eightfold Path means concentration on wholesome thoughts and actions. The Buddhist method of choice to develop right concentration is through the practice of meditation, single-pointed focus of attention.

11. Erwin Schrödinger, *Proceedings of the American Philosophical Society* 124 (1935).

12. Murti, *Central Philosophy*, p. 136.

13. Garfield, *Fundamental Wisdom of the Middle Way*, pp. 28–30.

14. Edward Conze, *Buddhist Thought in India*, London: George Allen & Unwin, 1962, p. 225.

15. Alan Watts, *The Way of Zen*, New York: Pantheon, 1957.

16. Murti, *Central Philosophy*, p. 219.

17. Th. Stcherbatsky, *The Conception of Buddhist Nirvana*, The Hague: Mouton, 1965, p. 69.

18. Foundation for Inner Peace, *A Course in Miracles*, Tiburon, CA: Foundation for Inner Peace, 1976.

PART TWO

A Guide to Naked Awareness

6

Introduction to Nonlocality and Nonduality

How is it that separation of awareness is an illusion? We live in a nonlocal reality, which is to say that we can be affected by events that are distant from our ordinary awareness. This is an alarming idea for those of us who do physics, because it means that laboratory experiments are subject to outside influences that may be beyond our control or knowledge. In fact, precognition research strongly suggests that an experiment could, in principle, be affected by a signal sent from the future! The eighteenth-century mystic William Blake famously described this so-called nonlocality by reminding us:

To see a world in a grain of sand; And a Heaven in a wild
    flower;
Hold infinity in the palm of your hand; And eternity in
    an hour.

In the twentieth century we would say nonlocality implies a fundamental connection or correlation betweens things and people that appear to be physically separated from one another. It's a connection that transcends and overcomes our old understanding of space-time separation.

The physics of nonlocality is fundamental to quantum theory. The most exciting research in physics today is the investigation of what physicist David Bohm calls *quantum-interconnectedness,* or nonlocal correlations. This idea was first described as quantum *entanglement* by Erwin Schrödinger in 1927. Then in 1935, Einstein, Podolsky, and Rosen (EPR) described entanglement as evidence of a "defect" in quantum theory. In the EPR paper, Einstein called this phenomenon a "ghostly" action at a distance.[1] The phenomenon greatly disturbed him because he thought it implied that messages could be sent faster than the speed of light, which is forbidden by his special relativity theory. And since there is evidence that we can know the future, the speed of thought is not only faster than the speed of light, but also immeasurable. This quantum entanglement was later formulated by J. S. Bell in 1964 as a mathematical proof of nonlocality and is at the very heart of the psychic abilities that we discuss later.[2]

To be specific, since Bell's theory, it has been repeatedly demonstrated that two quanta of light, given off from a single source and traveling at the speed of light in opposite directions, can maintain their connection to one another even at great distances. We find that such photons are instantly affected by what happens to their twin, even many kilometers away.

John Clauser and Stuart Freedman at the University of California at Berkeley were the first to demonstrate nonlocality in the laboratory.[3] They recently described their impressions of these experiments. Clauser told me (Targ) at a public meeting that "quantum interference experiments have been carried out with twin photons, electrons, atoms, and even large atomic structures such as 60-carbon-atom Bucky balls. It may be impossible to keep anything in a [local] box anymore." Clauser was referring to the familiar two-slit interference experiments that are usually done with light beams but are now also being done with all sorts of heavier and larger particles. In these two-slit interference experiments, the particles are directed toward a partition containing two slits. The particles may have passed through the right slit, the left slit, both slits, or neither. And there is absolutely no way to tell which slit they passed through, even when the particles are coming along one at a time. The indeterminacy illustrates the wave and particle nature of light. Thus these observations confirm the truth of Nagarjuna's formulation of "neither x nor not x." John Bell emphasized that "no theory of reality compatible with quantum theory can require spatially separate events to be independent." That is to say, the measurement of the polarization of one photon determines (or remains correlated with) the polarization of the other photon at its distant measurement site, no matter which way you turn the polarizer. This surprising coherence (or dependent coarising) between distant entities is commonly identified as "nonlocality" by Bell, Bohm, Clauser, and Freedman. Physicist Henry Stapp of the University of California at Berkeley states that these nonlocal quantum connections could be the "most important discovery in all of science."[4]

Nonlocality is a property of both time and space. It can be seen as representing the unified whole of space-time. Neils Bohr, who was the great conceptualizer of quantum physics, invented what he called "complementarity" as a nondual way to resolve the paradoxes of the dual wave nature and particle nature of light (and electrons also). Complementarity and Bohr's correspondence principle are ways of bridging the discrepancy between quantum and classical physics models (especially for large numbers). At the boundary of atomic physics, the quantum model and the classical model must agree. Classical models such as the orbital angular momentum of electrons must not be rendered absurd by the deeper model of quantum physics. The classical model actually works quite well in explaining the so-called "energy levels" of electrons, yet it fails to explain nonlocality and certain finer optical spectral observations.

Just as in the experiments with twin photons, some of the strongest data from psi research has been seen between identical twins, who seem to show the same kind of entanglement as the elementary particles. The English researcher Guy Playfair has recently published a book called *Twin Telepathy*, which is full of cases describing remarkable psychic connections between twins, who were often reared apart yet led amazingly similar lives.[5]

Studies of identical twins who were separated at birth and reared apart show that the twins nonetheless share striking similarities in their interests and experiences beyond what could be reasonably ascribed to their common DNA.

The following vivid example shows that nonlocality is not limited to atoms but can apply to human beings as well. One famous set of separated twins had both been named Jim by their adoptive parents. Although they never communicated with one another, each twin married a woman named Betty, divorced her, and then married a woman named Linda. When the brothers finally met as adults, it turned out that they were both firemen and had felt a compulsion to build a circular white bench around a tree in their respective backyards *just before coming to their first meeting at the University of Minnesota* (in the Twin Cities). There might be fireman genes, or music genes, but we do not think there are Linda genes, Betty genes, or white-bench genes. There's a nonlocal connection or resonance between the twin Jims, because they have trillions of identical DNA molecules in their bodies. They are coherent in the same way as two identical tuning forks tuned to the same note, where one will ring when the other is struck.

Recent research in areas as different as remote viewing, distant healing, and quantum physics correlates with the oldest spiritual teachings of the sages of India, who taught that "separation is an illusion." This concept suggests that there is no distance for consciousness and that we have an intuitive inner knowledge that transcends the conceptual limits of time and space. Three decades of research in remote viewing indicate that we all have a nonlocal perceptual ability available to us, should we decide to use it. This ability allows us to expand our awareness through space and time in order to describe and experience objects and events that are blocked from ordinary perception. This ability of the mind to extend itself is an indication of who we truly are; and with it comes the experience of Nagarjuna's four lemmas, wherein we become nondual participants in the universe as we break free of all artificial dualistic constraints.

Global Consciousness

Our individual awareness not only fills the globe, but is also interconnected with the awareness of all sentient beings. This would be the teaching of not only the Buddha, but also ongoing laboratory experiments in global consciousness. For several decades, physicist Helmut Schmidt has been investigating the surprising extent to which this consciousness can perturb the output of random number generators (RNGs). These delicate quantum devices normally produce random strings of 1s and 0s (+ or − electrical pulses) that have an unpredictable, but well ordered and balanced statistical distribution.[6]

Schmidt's successful experiments have led others to investigate whether the consciousness of a group would have an even greater effect on these devices. Dean Radin asked the question, "If the consciousness of one person could affect a random generator, what would be the effect of 500 million people all at the same time?" In 1995, the world's attention was focused on the murder trial of O. J. Simpson. Radin, at the University of Nevada, together with Roger Nelson at Princeton University and Dick Bierman at the University of Utrecht in The Hague, set up a total of five RNGs to investigate the possible change in world consciousness at the moment the jury delivered its verdict at the trial. As the pre-verdict television show came on the air at 9:00 A.M., there was a large increase in the coherence of the RNG output. This increase slowly returned to its normal randomness, where it remained for the balance of the hour. At ten o'clock, the foreman of the jury read the acquittal verdict. At that exact moment, all five of the RNGs shot up to unprecedented levels of coherent output, where they remained for several minutes, before decaying back to their normal values.[7]

Since this highly successful experiment, Roger Nelson has spearheaded the establishment of an array of more than 50 RNGs in widely separated global locations, all connected via the Internet. In this Global Consciousness Project, he has observed and recorded the coherent changes in the worldwide collection of RNG devices at moments of planetary coherence, attention, or calamity. Such significant planetary events have ranged from the funeral of Princess Diana to the tragedy of the destruction of the New York Twin Towers on 9/11. This latter is the largest and most statistically significant event ever recorded by the Global Consciousness devices. These findings were published in the prestigious journal *Foundations of Physics Letters.*[8] It is also interesting to note that there is a recurring global event recorded by the RNGs, namely, the annual worldwide New Year's Eve celebration. As the year changes in each time zone, the RNGs at that location each show their individual contribution to global festivities. It should be noted that although the O. J. verdict, Princess Diana's funeral, and the 9/11 tragedy each reached independent statistical significance, many other notable events were not individually significant. But the concatenation of all the events' deviations from chance is highly significant (odds of one in 30,000, for 185 events on the world scene). The Global Consciousness Program's website presents all their data and can be viewed at: http://noosphere.princeton.edu.

Schrödinger said that the teaching of our nonlocal nature, as it is reflected in the Hindu idea that Atman equals Brahman, "is the most profound idea in all of metaphysics."[9] As we described earlier, Atman is our personal self or soul, and Brahman is the entire physical and nonphysical universe. This remarkable Hindu teaching—from two millennia before Christ—declares that our personal awareness is nonlocal, fills all of space-time, and is one with it. That's who you are—limitless consciousness!

In the next chapter, we present contemporary laboratory data demonstrating that nonlocal awareness is real, not a metaphoric construct. This is where the wisdom teachers and the physicists can finally agree. Although we reside for a time as physical bodies, that is not the limit of who we are. *Our true self is nonlocal awareness.* This idea is not a matter of faith, but rather a direct experience available for those who would quiet their mind and explore the spaciousness of their own awareness.

Notes

1. A. Einstein, B. Podolsky, and N. Rosen, "Can a quantum mechanical description of physical reality be considered complete?" *Physical Review* 47 (1935), pp. 777–780.

2. J. S. Bell, "On the Einstein, Podolsky, Rosen paradox," *Physics* 1:1 (1964), pp. 195–200.

3. S. Freedman and J. Clauser, "Experimental test of local hidden variable theories," *Physical Review Letters* 28 (1972), pp. 934–941.

4. Henry Stapp, in Robert Nadeau and Menas Kafatos, *The Nonlocal Universe: The New Physics and Matters of the Mind*, New York: Oxford University Press, 1999.

5. Guy Lyon Playfair, *Twin Telepathy: The Psychic Connection*, London: Vega, 2002.

6. Helmut Schmidt, "Observation of a psychokinetic effect under highly controlled conditions," *Journal of Parapsychology* (1993), pp. 35–72. "Random generators and living systems as targets in retro-PK experiments," *Journal of the American Society for Psychical Research* 91:1 (1997), pp. 1–14.

7. Dean I. Radin, *The Conscious Universe*, New York: HarperEdge, 1997, p. 167.

8. R. Nelson, D. Radin, R. Shoup, and P. Bancel, "Correlations of continuous random data with major world events," *Foundations of Physics Letters* 15:6 (December 2002), pp. 537–550.

9. Erwin Schrödinger, *What Is Life? The Physical Aspect of the Living Cell*, Cambridge, England: Cambridge University Press, 1944.

7

Life in the Nonlocal World:
Experiencing Your Limitless Mind

Consciousness is a singular of which the plural is unknown.
There is only one thing, and that which seems to be a plurality is
merely a series of different aspects of this one thing, produced by
a deception, the Indian *maya*, as in a gallery of mirrors.
                                        —Erwin Schrödinger

It is now 30 years since the U.S. government initiated a program at Stanford Research Institute (SRI) in California, to investigate and apply psychic abilities. The program was called
remote viewing, which is the ability to perceive persons, places,
and events that are not within the range of the ordinary senses.

For more than two decades, this $20 million program, which began in 1972, received continuous financial and institutional support from the CIA, Air Force, Army Intelligence, and many other government agencies. One of the authors of this book, Russell Targ, was cofounder, along with Harold Puthoff, of this once-secret program. The findings were published in the world's most prestigious scientific journals: *Nature,*[1] *Proceedings of the Institute of Electrical and Electronics Engineers (IEEE),*[2] and *Proceedings of the American Association for the Advancement of Science* (AAAS).[3] The program also provided otherwise unavailable information to almost every branch of the U.S. intelligence community. Just a few of our exploits include finding a downed Soviet bomber with atomic weapons on board that had crashed in Africa, tracking the health of American prisoners in the Iran hostage situation, and describing details of a failed Chinese atomic bomb test. The program was terminated at the end of the Cold War in 1995, when the government decided that the United States no longer had any serious enemies.

Remote viewing has now been demonstrated in many U.S. and international laboratories and is an experiential example of nonlocality and expanded consciousness. In our SRI investigations into remote viewing, people were able to envision distant places, as well as future events and activities. Our task was to learn to understand psychic abilities and to use these abilities to gather information about the Soviet Union, China, Iran, and many other countries of concern during the Cold War. Although we initially worked with known psychics, we have since found from years of experience that most people can quickly learn to do remote viewing. And they frequently can incorporate this direct knowing of the world—both present and future—into their lives.

Nevertheless, throughout Western culture there is great cognitive dissonance over psychic abilities. People experience it yet deny it. A recent (June 2001) Gallup poll indicated that more than half of the U.S. population feel that they are having psychic experiences. Reporting these ubiquitous experiences, however, is still strongly repressed in this society, and in mainstream media. But Google has 962,000 "remote viewing" hits!

Researcher Louisa Rhine found that by far the most common psychic event to appear in the life of the average person is the precognitive dream.[4] These dreams give us a glimpse of events that we will experience in the future. From hundreds of laboratory experiments at Princeton University as well as at SRI, it is evident that precognition occurs. And we consider it important to note that precognition is just as successful and reliable as ordinary real-time ESP (extrasensory perception).[5] To know whether or not a dream is precognitive, you must recognize whether it is caused by the mental residue of the past day or by deeply held wishes or anxieties. Precognitive dreams are distinguished by an unusual clarity and they often contain bizarre or unfamiliar material. Dream experts like to speak of their preternatural clarity. These are not wish-fulfillment or anxiety dreams. For example, if you are unprepared for an exam and dream about failing it, we would not consider that to be precognition, but ordinary cause and effect. On the other hand, if you have taken hundreds of plane flights over many years, and then have a frightening dream about a crash, you might want to rethink your travel plans. During the SRI remote-viewing program, our contract monitor from the CIA saved his life by rescheduling a planned flight out of Detroit after he had a particularly vivid and frightening dream of being in a plane crash. Subsequently, he witnessed the actual crash of that flight firsthand.

Unfortunately, his partner was on the flight and died. He failed to tell his partner about the dream because he didn't want to seem superstitious.

We now know that information from the future regularly filters into our dreams. One could reasonably say that these precognitive dreams indicate that the future affects our past; that is, our dream tonight may sometimes be caused by an event that we will experience at a later time. This idea strongly violates our ordinary understanding of causality. But it is an example of why Nagarjuna argues against linear causality and in favor of *mutual coarising*. Events can happen in the present or in the future, but it's frequently impossible to determine whether the actual causal elements occurred now or then.

Experimental data from many laboratories demonstrate that psi performance is not a function of either spatial or temporal distance. It is no harder to describe a hidden target across the planet than to describe something across the street. Similarly, the future is just as accessible as the present. This is what we mean by a nonlocal ability, or nonlocal awareness, which is another aspect of who we are. This further confirms Nagarjuna's teaching that nothing exists independently in the world, and that we are all connected to one another and to nature by our thoughts and by nonlocal space-time.

The implications of research in psi abilities illuminate our observation that we live in a profoundly interconnected world. As described in the previous chapter, the most exciting research in quantum physics today is the investigation of what physicist David Bohm calls quantum-interconnectedness or nonlocal correlations.[6] If laboratories around the world can demonstrate that quanta of light emitted in opposite directions at the speed of light maintain their connection to one another, why is it so difficult to accept that people and the world around us may have our own interconnectedness, perhaps sharing a collective consciousness?[7]

Interconnectedness

Remote viewers can often experience and describe a hidden object or a remote natural or architectural site, based on the presence of a cooperative person at the distant location. They are able to do the same when presented with geographical coordinates of latitude and longitude or some other target demarcation, which we call an "address." Remote viewers can describe shape, form, and color much more reliably than the target's name, function, or other analytical information. In addition to vivid visual imagery, viewers sometimes describe associated feelings, sounds, smells, and even electrical or magnetic fields. Blueprint accuracy has occasionally been achieved in these double-blind experiments, and reliability in a series can be as high as 80 percent, especially with an experienced viewer.

With practice, people become increasingly able to separate the psychic signal from the distracting mental noise of memory, analysis, naming, judgment, and imagination. Targets and target details as small as one millimeter can be sensed. Moreover, again and again, we have seen that accuracy and resolution of remote-viewing targets are not sensitive to variations in distance. In 1984, my daughter Elisabeth and I organized a pair of successful remote-viewing experiments performed in Moscow under the auspices and control of the USSR Academy of Sciences. Famed Russian healer Djuna Davitashvili was asked to describe where an SRI colleague would be hiding in San Francisco, California, at a specific time. In this precognitive experiment, she had to focus her attention six thousand miles to the west and two hours into the future in order to describe his location correctly. Elisabeth interviewed Djuna in Russian, as Djuna drew a picture of trapezoid-shaped buildings and "some sort of cupola," as well as a large animal with glass eyes. In fact, the SRI colleague in California was standing in front of the merry-go-round on Pier 37, and the trapezoid-shaped buildings and merry-go-round animals with glass eyes were evident in the photo of the target site, shown to Djuna later. The only other time a viewer mentioned a "cupola" in a remote-viewing session was when the target was a merry-go-round, this time in Palo Alto, California.

Another clearly documented demonstration took place ten years earlier. In 1974, Hal Puthoff and I (Targ) carried out a demonstration of psychic abilities for the CIA in which Pat Price, a highly psychic retired police commissioner, described the contents and activities inside and outside of a secret Soviet weapons laboratory in the far reaches of Soviet Siberia. Price was given only the geographical coordinates of latitude and longitude for a reference, that is, with no on-site cooperation from a person at the target. This experiment was such a stunning success that we were personally forced to undergo a formal congressional investigation by the House Committee on Intelligence Oversight to determine if there had been a breach in national security. We went to Washington, D.C., for the interrogation. Of course, no breach was found, and the government supported our research into psychic functioning for another 20 years.

During these experiments at SRI, Pat Price and I sat in an electrically shielded room as Price made the sketch shown here, illustrating his mental impressions of a giant gantry crane that he psychically "saw" rolling back and forth overhead as he lay on the roof of a building at the target site!

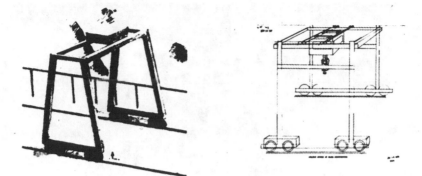

Above right is Pat Price's drawing of his psychic impressions of a gantry crane at the secret Soviet research and development site at Semipalatinsk, showing remarkable similarity to a later CIA drawing based on satellite photography shown at left. Note, for example, that both cranes have eight wheels.

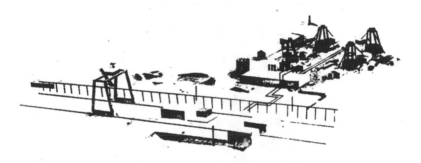

Here is a CIA artist tracing of a satellite photograph of the Semipalatinsk target site. Such tracings were made by the CIA to conceal the accuracy of our satellite photography at that time.

Data from formal and controlled SRI investigations were highly statistically significant—thousands of times greater than chance expectation—for each series of trials, and have been widely published. (The 20 years of remote-viewing research conducted for the CIA and the Moscow to San Francisco experiment

This is a 1974 photograph of the cofounders of the SRI program, taken at a small airport, after a remote-viewing experiment from a glider. From left, Hal Puthoff, Russell Targ, CIA contract monitor Kit Green, and psychic police commissioner Pat Price

are outlined in my coauthored book *Miracles of Mind: Exploring Nonlocal Consciousness and Spiritual Healing*.)[8]

During one experimental series at SRI, I (Targ) was working with Pat Price, who did not arrive one day for the scheduled trial. So, in the spirit of "the show must go on," I spontaneously decided to undertake the remote viewing myself. Prior to that, I had been only an interviewer and facilitator for such trials. In this series, we were trying to describe the day-to-day activities of Hal Puthoff as he traveled through Colombia, in South America. We would not receive any feedback until he returned, and I therefore had no clues at all as to what he was doing. I closed my eyes for my first remote-viewing trial and immediately had an image of an island airport. The surprisingly accurate sketch I drew is shown here. What we learned from this trial is that even a scientist can be psychic, when the necessity level is high enough!

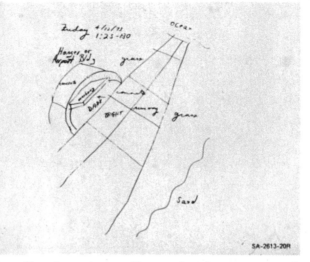

Sketch produced by physicist Russell Targ when he spontaneously took the role of remote viewer in the absence of psychic Pat Price.

This photograph shows the target, which was an airport on an island off San Andreas, Colombia. Targ correctly saw "ocean at the end of a runway."

For a phenomenon thought in many circles not to exist, a great deal is certainly known about how to increase and decrease ESP's accuracy and reliability. The sensitivity to the presence of a greater awareness allows some individuals to mentally choreograph their feelings into a new understanding and meaning of life. Once the existence of psychic ability has been internalized, it can't help but change and expand the idea of who we really are. In fact, in remote viewing, it appears that the ordinary reality we perceive is not one universe but a spiderweb of timeless interactions (a kind of nonlocal signaling) in which the future appears to be tugging on the present in order to become actualized.

Why Bother with Psi Research and Remote Viewing?

We now know that we can use our remote-viewing abilities to look at a distance and into the future as well. We can find our missing car keys and elusive parking spaces. We can even psychically forecast changes in the stock market, which a number of people have done successfully. But the authors are confident that the highest use of these abilities is to experience who we really are, and that *who we are* is limitless awareness that fills all of space and time.

The data of psi research demonstrate that we are capable of expanded awareness far beyond our physical bodies. That is to say, who we are could not possibly be just a physical body, but, rather, we are nonlocal awareness residing for the moment as a physical body. The body is just a temporary address. In fact, the principal finding of remote-viewing research is that there is not yet any known spatial or temporal limit to our awareness. In consciousness, there is only one of us here. Or as Buddhists and quantum physicists tirelessly remind us, "Separation is an illusion."

This is exactly what the great contemporary psychic Ingo Swann teaches regarding remote viewing. Swann further developed this psychic ability when we worked together at Stanford Research Institute. He showed us that we must overcome memory, imagination, and analysis in order to see into the distance and the future. He called these obstacles or obscurations *analytical overlay* (AOL). They are exactly the hindrances described 1,800 years earlier by the sage Nagarjuna. The understanding of these hindrances to naked awareness is one of the oldest ideas to appear in any spiritual literature. Overcoming our mental chatter invites us to become part of a pure stream of consciousness—interconnected with all of life—bringing the Atman and Brahman together in both the physical and metaphysical universe.

The revered Hindu sage Patanjali of the fourth century B.C. had a similar teaching in his sutras.[9] The famous Sutras of Patanjali begin with the line, "Yoga is mind wave quieting." For him, yoga was union with God or all eternity. He wrote that when you quiet your mind, you have an opportunity to see into the distance and into the future. You can diagnose illness and heal the sick. But these *siddhis*, or powers, he described were not the objective of his teaching. He was much more interested in furthering self-realization than self-improvement. These powers were merely an indication that a student was on the right path and making progress with his or her mind-quieting meditation on a single-pointed focus of attention. If the powers are viewed as an end in themselves, or as an accomplishment, then they become a stumbling block to discovering one's true nature.

The twentieth century has witnessed a progression toward more of a consciousness-centric science. From the paradigm-shattering realizations of Planck, Bohr, Schrödinger, and other great quantum physicists working in the first few decades of the twentieth century, we learned that we cannot remove ourselves from any events in our space-time manifold. Our presence as observers affects everything around us, and we must always question how our *intention* imprints itself on reality. The observer always affects whatever he or she is observing.

An understanding of our unlimited abilities to see universally was also explained as early as the ninth century, when the great Buddhist teacher Padmasambhava taught that when we give up seeing the world though our conditioning, we have an opportunity to experience our lives in liberation and spaciousness. Known also as Guru Rinpoche, Padmasambhava was the historical figure who brought Buddhism from India to Tibet. In his inspiring and powerful book, *Self-Liberation through Seeing with Naked Awareness,* he teaches that we tend to see the world through the lens of all our past sufferings, betrayals, and instructions.[10] He writes that when we finally give up this conditioned awareness in favor of naked awareness—free of judgment, fear, and resentment—then we are on the path to timeless existence and liberation. This is a teaching that is nondual, in that it is nonjudgmental and nonconceptual. We must give up naming and grasping in order to see truly. This is the path to true freedom, spaciousness, and the end of suffering.

Notes

1. R. Targ and H. Puthoff, "Information transfer under conditions of sensory shielding," *Nature* 251 (1974), pp. 602–607.

2. R. Targ and H. E. Puthoff, "A perceptual channel for information transfer over kilometer distances: Historical perspective and recent research," *Proceedings of the IEEE [Institute of Electrical and Electronics Engineers]* 64:3 (1976).

3. H. E. Puthoff, R. Targ, and E. C. May, "Experimental psi research: Implications for physics," in R. G. Jahn, *The Role of*

Consciousness in the Physical World, AAAS [American Association for the Advancement of Science] Selected Symposium 57, Boulder, CO: Westview Press, 1981, pp. 37–86.

4. L. Rhine, "Frequency and types of experience in spontaneous precognition," *Journal of Parapsychology* 8 (1954), pp. 93–123.

5. Robert G. Jahn and Brenda J. Dunne, *Margins of Reality: The Role of Consciousness in the Physical World*, San Diego, CA: Harcourt, Brace, Jovanovich, 1987.

6. David Bohm and B. J. Hiley, *The Undivided Universe: An Ontological Interpretation of Quantum Theory*, New York: Routledge, 1993.

7. S. Freedman and J. Clauser, "Experimental test of local hidden variable theories," *Physical Review Letters* 28 (1972), pp. 934–941. W. Tittel, J. Brendel, H. Zbinden, and N. Gisin, "Violation of Bell inequalities by photons more than 10 km apart," *Physical Review Letters* 81:17 (1998), pp. 3563–3566.

8. Russell Targ and Jane Katra, *Miracles of Mind: Exploring Nonlocal Consciousness and Spiritual Healing*, Novato, CA: New World Library, 1998.

9. Swami Prabhavananda and Christopher Isherwood (trans.), *How to Know God*, Hollywood, CA: Vedanta Press, 1983.

10. Padmasambhava, *Self-Liberation through Seeing with Naked Awareness*, tr. John Myrdhin Reynolds, Ithaca, NY: Snow Lion Publications, 2000.

NOTE: Coauthor Dr. J. J. Hurtak has never been in consultation with nor employed by the CIA.

8

Healing the World with
Your Nonlocal Mind

After scrutinizing this body of data for almost two decades,
I have come to regard it as one of the best kept secrets in medical science. I'm convinced that the distant, nonlocal effects are
real and that healing happens.

—Dr. Larry Dossey

In remote viewing, we expand our awareness to experience
the broader world around us. Expanding further, we discover
that we can actually create an effect in some places that we previously had just been viewing. We call this nonlocal effect "distant intentionality." More than 30 years of investigations clearly

show that one person's thoughts can affect the physiological functioning of another, distant person. Not only can we inflow information about the distant world, but we can also outflow our healing intentions to relieve suffering and reduce pain.

We do not yet understand the causal mechanism involved, but the results are indisputable and have obvious implications for our ability to facilitate healing in others. This healing, whether in the laboratory or in a clinical setting, as Larry Dossey proposes, is considered to be nonlocal because the efficacy of the healing or mental influence is independent of distance. We take for granted the calming effects that a mother's gentle cooing has on her distressed infant, not really thinking about the effects of her soothing intentions. But how do we know that our thoughts affect others? A significant body of research now exists demonstrating that one person's focused intentions can directly influence the physiological processes of someone far away. "Do unto others as you would have them do unto you" takes on urgent meaning when we realize that we are all truly connected, and perhaps even "entangled," as the physicists say.

Experiencing the Future

In the laboratory, we know that if we show a frightening picture to a person, there will be a significant change in his or her physiology. Blood pressure, heart rate, and skin resistance will all change. This fight-or-flight reaction is called an "orienting response." Researcher Dean Radin, while at the University of Nevada, has shown that this orienting response is also observed in a person's physiology a few seconds *before* they witness the scary picture, even though they don't know when or what they will be shown.[1] In balanced, double-blind experiments, Radin, currently senior scientist at the Institute of Noetic Sciences, has demonstrated that if you are about to see scenes of sexuality, violence, or mayhem, your body will steel itself against the future shock or insult. But if you are about to see a picture of a wastebasket or a flower garden, then there is no such strong anticipatory reaction. Here, it seems, one's direct physical perception of the shocking picture, when it occurs, causes one to have a unique—*three seconds earlier*—physical response. Our future is actually affecting our past! Interestingly, fear is much easier to measure physiologically than bliss. (If ESP were an electromagnetic phenomenon, this could be described as an advanced wave.)[2] These intriguing experiments are also described in Radin's comprehensive book *The Conscious Universe*.

The pictures that Radin uses in his experiments are from a standardized and quantified set of emotional stimuli used in psychology research. These pictures range from downhill skiing or nudes on the beach on the positive side, to car crashes and abdominal surgery, generally considered to elicit a negative emotional response. Pictures of paper cups and fountain pens are found in the neutral range. The exciting result Radin reports is that the more emotional the picture shown to the subject at a later time, the greater in magnitude is the subject's response before seeing the picture. Radin reports this correlation to be significant, at odds greater than one in a hundred. Professor Dick Bierman at Utrecht University in Holland has successfully replicated Radin's findings, even though he had to assemble a more sexually explicit set of pictures in order to psychically excite his Amsterdam college students.

Even stronger results have been obtained by physicists Edwin May and James Spottiswoode, who measure the galvanic skin response of subjects who are about to hear a loud noise in their earphones at randomly selected intervals. Again, measurements from more than 100 participants show that their nervous system seems to know three to five seconds in advance when it will be assaulted with a disagreeable stimulus. It is as though our physiological "now" has a three-second temporal span. When I (Targ) was a subject in Ed May's experiment, my responses showed a steady decline. This was because, after a few loud and annoying bursts of sound, my subconscious figured out that these sounds were not actually going to hurt me. At that point, I began to doze off into meditation, even with occasional loud noises in my earphones.

The most significant evidence for the so-called prestimulus response comes, however, from the Hungarian researcher Zoltán Vassy. He administered painful electric shocks as the stimulus to be precognized. His results are the strongest of all, because the human body does not habituate to electric shocks. One always experiences electric shocks as a new and alarming stimulus, even though the shock resides in one's future.[3]

We would say that this is a case in which your direct physical perception of the electric shock or picture, when it occurs, causes you to have a unique physical response *at an earlier time.* Your annoying future is affecting your physiological past. Psychologist William Braud, in his excellent book *Distant Mental Influence,* describes these experiments as follows.

Although this presentiment effect is usually taken to reflect precognition (future-knowing) operating at an unconscious body level, these interesting findings can just as well be interpreted as instances in which objective events (the presentation of the slide itself or the person's future reaction to the slide) may be acting backward in time to influence the person's physiological activity.[4]

Exciting experiments in the area of Distant Mental Influence of Living Systems (DMILS) have been carried out by William Braud at the Institute of Transpersonal Psychology in Palo Alto, California, and by anthropologist Marilyn Schlitz, research director at the Institute of Noetic Sciences.[5] They have repeatedly shown that if a person, sitting as a sender, simply *attends fully* to a distant person whose physiological activity is being monitored, the sender can influence the distant person's autonomic galvanic skin responses. In four separate experiments involving 78 sessions, a sender-participant staring intently at a closed-circuit TV monitor image of a distant receiver-participant was able to influence significantly the remote person's electrodermal response (galvanic skin response [GSR]). In these cases, no techniques of intentional focusing or mental imaging were used by the influencer. The influencer simply stared at the "staree's" image on the video screen during the 30-second trials, which were randomly interspersed with control periods.

In these studies, Braud and Schlitz discovered something just as interesting as this telepathically induced effect on our unconscious system. They found that the most anxious and introverted people had the greatest magnitudes of unconscious electrodermal responses when their video images were being stared at. In other words, more shy and introverted people reacted with significantly more stress to being stared at than did the sociable and extroverted people. Quiet introverts may possess more sensitivity of consciousness than others. This experiment gives scientific validation to the common human experience of feeling that you are being stared at, and turning around to find that someone is, indeed, staring at you. For example, men know that in church or the theater they can cause a woman to turn around and look in their direction by staring intently at the back of her neck. These examples show that one person's thoughts can affect another's physiology.

Distant Healing

From the dawn of history, certain individuals have been recognized as possessing special healing gifts. The pharaohs of ancient Egypt viewed healers as revered advisors. Healers founded the world's great religions: Buddha, Jesus of Nazareth, and the prophet Muhammad were all said to be gifted healers. Centuries before Jesus, the Hebrew prophets Elijah, Elisha, and Isaiah were acknowledged healers; and Moses was able to heal Israelites from serpent bites (Num. 21:6–9). Medicine men and healing shamans throughout Africa, Asia, and the Americas held some of the most esteemed positions in their tribes. In contrast, Western thought and allopathic medicine have largely ignored the broad range of mind-to-mind healing that has been effective in other cultures. With our reverence for Humanism and Reason, we have much to relearn about the role of consciousness in healing. Only now, through use of the scientific method, are we realizing the power of the mind to heal. In recent years, a number of pioneering experiments have explored the role that one person's consciousness may have on another person's health and discovered that there is a physiological connection that spans space and time.[6]

In his 1993 book *Healing Research,* psychiatrist Daniel Benor examined more than 150 controlled studies from around the world. He reviewed psychic, mental, and spiritual healing experiments done on a variety of living organisms: enzymes, cell cultures, bacteria, yeasts, plants, animals, and humans. More than half of the studies demonstrate significant healing.[7]

An experiment of this type was carried out in the 1980s, in which a healer was able to prolong the life of bacteria that were challenged by antibiotics. Physicist Elizabeth Rauscher and biologist Beverly Rubik, both of the University of California at Berkeley, worked with the legendary American healer Olga Worrall.[8] As a healer, Mrs. Worrall refused to consciously harm any living thing, but she was willing to attempt to heal *E. coli* bacteria that had been poisoned with tetracycline. In well-controlled side-by-side comparison tests, the two researchers showed that Mrs. Worrall was able to keep alive the *E. coli* cells toward which she was directing her healing thoughts for a longer period of time than the controls. After four hours of exposure to the antibiotic, all of the control bacteria were dead, while a significant number of bacteria for which she had been praying lived on. An important finding from this study was that the healer was not able to increase the reproduction rate of the healthy bacteria colony. Rather, she was able to aid the bacteria that were in need of healing.

Researcher William Braud was always very selective in the systems he studied. If the creatures were not labile enough, or too sluggish, it might be too difficult to get them started. If an animal's normal behavior is very near the activity ceiling, then the animal may be showing nearly all the action you can expect from it. For instance, a gerbil would be a better target than a snail, slug, hummingbird, or bee. It would be very hard to get the snail's attention, and similarly difficult to increase the activity level of the hummingbird.

Although most of Braud's highly successful work involved increasing and decreasing the degree of relaxation of people at a distant location, one of his most important experiments involved trying to come psychically to the aid of threatened red blood cells. In all the other experiments he did with living systems, the creature (even the goldfish) had a level of consciousness that could, in principle, be affected by a distant person.[9] In other experiments, subjects in the laboratory were asked to influence the behavior of red blood cells, which to the best of our knowledge have not shown any independent consciousness. In these studies, the cells were put into test tubes of distilled water, which is a toxic environment for them. If the salt content of the solution deviates too much from that of blood plasma, the cell wall weakens and the contents of the cell go into solution. This unfortunate situation is dispassionately called *hemolysis*. The degree of hemolysis is easily measured, since the transmission of light through a solution containing intact blood cells is much less than through a solution of dissolved cells. A spectrophotometer is used to measure the light transmission as a function of time during the experiment.

In each series, with 32 different subjects, 20 tubes of blood were compared for each person. The subjects, situated in a distant room, had the task of attempting to save from aqueous destruction the little corpuscles in ten of the target tubes. The blood cells in the ten control tubes had to fend for themselves. Braud found that the people working as remote healers were able to retard significantly the hemolysis of the blood in the tubes they were trying to protect. And they were even more successful at retarding the hemolysis in the blood they personally contributed.

Bacteria are much smaller than red blood cells, but they have a nucleus and are able to reproduce, so they have a more complex system than blood cells do. Both of these one-celled systems are alive, and we can therefore imagine their having an interaction with human consciousness. Similar experiments have been carried out, however, with ordinary distilled water as the target for healing change. A mental influence over the state of a nonliving system such as water implies direct psychic interaction with a part of the physical universe, as the following studies demonstrate.

The results of a most important landmark study by Fred Sicher, psychiatrist Elisabeth Targ, and others at California Pacific Medical Center in San Francisco were published in the December 1998 issue of the *Western Journal of Medicine*.[10] The study investigated the positive therapeutic effects of distant healing, or healing intentionality, on men with advanced AIDS. In this highly regarded medical journal, the researchers defined nonlocal or distant healing as an act of "mentation intended to benefit another person's physical and/or emotional well-being at a distance." They also noted that this has been found in some form in nearly every culture since prehistoric time. Their research hypothesized that an intensive ten-week distant healing intervention by experienced healers located around the United States would benefit the medical outcomes for a population of advanced AIDS patients in the San Francisco area.

The researchers performed two separate, randomized, double-blind studies: a pilot study involving 20 male subjects stratified by the number of AIDS-defining illnesses, and a replication study of 40 men carefully matched into pairs by age, T-cell count, and number of AIDS-defining illnesses. The participants' conditions were assessed by psychometric testing and blood testing three times: at their enrollment, after the distant-healing intervention, and six months later when physicians reviewed their medical charts. In the pilot study, four of the ten control subjects died, whereas *all the subjects* in the treatment group survived. But this result may have been confounded by unequal age distributions in the two groups.

In the second study, men with AIDS were again recruited from the San Francisco Bay Area. They were told that they had a 50-50 chance of being in the treatment group, versus the control group. All subjects were pair-matched for age, CD4 count, and AIDS-defining diseases.

Forty distant healers from all parts of the country— Christian, Jewish, Buddhist, Native American, and shamanic traditions, in addition to secular "bioenergetic" schools—took part in the study. Each of them had more than five years of experience in their particular form of healing. Each subject in the healing group was treated by a total of ten different healers on a rotating healing.schedule. Healers were asked to work on their assigned subject for approximately one hour per day for six consecutive days, with instructions to "direct an intention of health and well-being" to the subject to whom they were attending. None of the 40 subjects in the study ever met the healers, nor did they or the experimenters know into which group anyone had been randomized.

By the midpoint of the study, neither group of subjects was able significantly to guess whether or not they were in the healing group. By the end of the study, however, there were many fewer opportunistic illnesses, which allowed the healing group to be able to identify itself—with significant odds against chance! Since all subjects were being treated with triple-drug therapy, there were no deaths in either group. The treatment group experienced significantly better medical and quality-of-life outcomes (odds of 100 to 1) on many quantitative measures, including fewer outpatient doctor visits (185 vs. 260); fewer days of hospitalization (10 vs. 68); less severe illnesses acquired during the study, as measured by illness severity scores (16 vs. 43); and significantly less emotional distress. In the study, Dr. Elisabeth Targ concluded, "Decreased hospital visits, fewer severe new diseases, and greatly improved subjective health supports the hypothesis of positive therapeutic effects of distant healing."

The editor of the journal introduced the paper thus: "The paper published below is meant to advance science and debate. It has been reviewed, revised, and re-reviewed by nationally known experts in biostatistics and complementary medicine . . . We have chosen to publish this provocative paper to stimulate other studies of distant healing, and other complementary practices and agents. It is time for more light, less dark, less heat."

Two other studies of distant healing have been published in prestigious medical journals. In 1988, physician Randolph Byrd published in the *Southern Medical Journal* a successful double-blind demonstration of distant healing. The study involved 393 cardiac patients at San Francisco General Hospital.[11] And in 1999, cardiologist William Harris of the University of Missouri in Kansas City published a similar successful study with 990 heart patients. His paper appeared in the *Archives of Internal Medicine*.[12]

The outcomes of all three clinical experiments departed significantly from chance expectation. The work of Sicher, Targ, and colleagues, however, required fewer than one-tenth the number of patients to achieve this significance. We attribute this greater effect size ($Z/N^{1/2}$, where Z is the departure from chance expectation and N is the number of trials) to the fact that Sicher and Targ worked with healers who each had more than five years of healing experience, whereas the others worked with well-intentioned, but much less experienced people. (There's no substitute for practice.)

A detailed analysis of 23 clinical studies of intercessory prayer and distant healing has recently been published by John Astin and colleagues in the *Annals of Internal Medicine*.[13] An examination of 16 studies with adequate double-blind designs showed significant effect size of 0.4, with an overall significance of $P < 10^{-4}$ for 2,139 patients. In addition, two excellent analyses of distant intentionality and distant healing studies have been published by pioneering researchers Marilyn Schlitz, William Braud, and Elisabeth Targ.[14]

Taking cognizance of the nonlocal nature of our universe, Braud has recently conjectured in *Alternative Therapies* that our *healing intentions* may achieve their goal by reaching backward in time to affect the critical "seed moments" in alternate future pathways of the development of the illness. Braud suggests that these seed moments may be more labile—fluttering like aspen leaves—and hence they may be more susceptible avenues of change in intercessory distant healing.[15] The healing intention can affect the fluttering seed moment at an earlier time. This idea of *backward causation* is like the previously described experience of precognitive dreams, in which our dream in the night is ostensibly "caused" by the confirmatory experience that we typically have the next day.

The Speed of Thought

As soon as we suspend our conditioned awareness, we have the opportunity to experience healing abilities in our lives. When we begin to reside in spaciousness, we become aware that anyone's suffering is reflected in our own suffering. The result is that none of us will be entirely free of suffering until we are all free of suffering. None get out of hell until we all do. As long as large numbers of people in the world feel frustrated, hopeless, angry, and hungry, there can never be peace.

With the understanding that the fundamental nature of nonlocality is expressed in the universe through quantum physics, as well as psi phenomena, we begin to comprehend the universality of consciousness. The psi database and the fundamental properties of nonlocality in physics lead us inexorably to the conclusion that the speed of thought is transcendent to any finite velocity. Velocity is defined as the distance something travels divided by the time it took to get there ($V = d/t$). In other words, the speed of something is measured by how long it takes to get from here to there. Because precognition occurs when the event is experienced *prior* to its apparent cause, the speed of thought appears to be instantaneous or any other velocity one chooses—even negative velocity—because the *perception* occurs before the event! The speed of thought is therefore undefined in meters per second. Because consciousness can access nonlocal space-time as though it were contiguous, space-time distances are nonexistent for mind-to-mind or mind-to-target awareness. Separation of consciousness is thus an illusion. Since there is no velocity and no distance for consciousness (your awareness and my awareness), there can be no separation.

In this context, Nagarjuna would have us understand that thought is the necessary violation of so-called objective structure, and that the all-pervasiveness of mind permits one to work with thought instantaneously in any direction. The compelling data for precognition make it appear that the future is unalterably determined. This fatalist point of view maintains that our awareness creeps inexorably along the time line at a rate of one second per second, and time is measured by events along this line. But this seeming limitation of our free will is only a four-space perception (ordinary space-time: x,y,z + time). If you move your awareness off the ordinary plane of awareness into nonlocal, and probably complex, space-time, then you can experience free will concomitant with naked awareness. Otherwise our activity is driven by the ordinary deterministic causality of our conditioned lives. We believe that the higher-dimensional space described elsewhere by Rauscher and Targ explains psychic entanglement and gives additional degrees of freedom that are available to our awareness, allowing us to have greater access to possible futures.[16]

Notes

1. Dean I. Radin, *The Conscious Universe*, New York: HarperEdge, 1997.

2. All electromagnetic radiation is described by formulations called Maxwell's equations. These equations have positive and negative solutions. The negative solution, called the retarded potential, shows that effects occur after the movement of an electron. The other, advanced potential suggests that effects can occur in anticipation of this movement. The physicist P. A. M. Dirac uses this advanced wave in his widely accepted model of the electron.

3. Zoltán Vassy, "Method for measuring the probability of 1 bit extrasensory information transfer between living organisms," *Journal of Parapsychology* 42 (1978), pp. 158–160.

4. William Braud, *Distant Mental Influence: Its Contributions to Science, Healing, and Human Interactions*, Charlottesville, VA: Hampton Roads, 2003, p. xxxv.

5. W. G. Braud and M. J. Schlitz, "Consciousness interactions with remote biological systems: Anomalous intentionality effects," *Subtle Energies* 2:1 (1991), pp. 1–46.

6. The healing material in this chapter is based on Jane Katra and Russell Targ, *Heart of the Mind*, Novato, CA: New World Library, 1999.

7. Daniel J. Benor, *Spiritual Healing: Scientific Validation of a Healing Revolution [Healing Research, Vol. 1]*, Southfield, MI: Vision Publications, 2001.

8. B. Rubik and E. Rauscher, "Effects on motility behavior and growth rate of *Salmonella typhimurium* in the presence of a psychic subject," in W. G. Roll (ed.), *Research in Parapsychology*, Metuchen, NJ: Scarecrow Press,

1979, pp. 140–142. Ambrose Worrall, in Harold Sherman, *Your Power to Heal,* New York: Harper & Row, 1972.

9. W. Braud, "Direct mental influence on the rate of hemolysis of human red blood cells," *Journal of the American Society for Psychical Research* (January 1990), pp. 1–24. All of the references to the work of William Braud can also be found in his book *Distant Mental Influence.*

10. F. Sicher, E. Targ, D. Moore, and H. Smith, "A randomized double-blind study of the effect of distant healing in a population with advanced AIDS," *Western Journal of Medicine* 169 (December 1998), pp. 356–363.

11. R. Byrd, "Positive therapeutic effects of intercessory prayer in a coronary care unit population," *Southern Medical Journal* 81:7 (July 1988), pp. 826–829.

12. W. S. Harris et al., "A randomized, controlled trial of the effects of remote intercessory prayer on outcomes in patients admitted to the coronary care unit," *Archives of Internal Medicine* 159 (October 25, 1999), pp. 2273–2278.

13. J. A. Astin, E. Harkness, and E. Ernst, "The efficacy of 'distant healing': A systematic review of randomized trials," *Annals of Internal Medicine* 132:11 (June 2000), pp. 903–910.

14. M. Schlitz and W. Braud, "Distant intentionality and healing: Assessing the evidence," *Alternative Therapies in Health and Medicine* 3:6 (November 1997). E. Targ, "Evaluating distant healing: A research review," *Alternative Therapies in Health and Medicine* 3:6 (November 1997). On the other hand, a large study of intercessory prayer carried out by Dr. Mitchell Koucoff at Duke University in 2003 failed to find significant healing. The study used totally inexperienced "congregational healing" (*Lancet,* July 16, 2005).

15. W. Braud, "Wellness implications of retroactive intentional influence: Exploring an outrageous hypothesis," *Alternative Therapies in Health and Medicine* 6:1 (2000), pp. 37–48.

16. E. A. Rauscher and R. Targ, "The speed of thought: Investigation of a complex space-time metric to describe psychic phenomena," *Journal of Scientific Exploration* 15:3 (Fall 2001), pp. 331–354. Online at www.espresearch.com.

9

The Nature of New Identity: The Universal Self

The meaning of your life depends on which ideas you permit to use you. Who you think you are determines where you put your attention. Where you direct your attention creates your life experiences, and brings a new course of events into being. Where you habitually put your attention is what you worship. What do you worship in this mindstream called your life?

—Gangaji

Plainly speaking, ignorance is the source of all our suffering—ignorance of who we are. The solution to one's suffering is to discover, first and foremost, who is suffering. For Ramana Maharshi, the twentieth-century Indian sage, all troubles reduce to one trouble:

mistaken identity. For example, there is no greater absurdity than to imagine that who you are is who you see in the mirror in the morning. When we investigate "Who am I?" we discover that the "I" is just the story of *me*. The self that is seeking to become realized is the substrate of the individual. It is our limitless nonlocal awareness that is beginning to notice its connection to the infinite and the absolute. To discover this self, you don't have to go anywhere. Better not to go. Just be still. You don't have to change anything. Just be still and surrender to the love that is inside, trying to get your attention. By the eighth century, Dzogchen Buddhist teachers were telling us that who we are is the pristine energy of unconditional love without an object (*vajra,* heart essence). The teaching is that when we finally stop our ongoing mental chatter, we can experience the flow of loving awareness, which is who we are. The eighth-century Buddhist master Shantideva teaches that there is no externally existing place called heaven or hell; our reality is a perception of our state of mind.

There are three main strands of Buddhism. *Hinayana* Buddhism (the lesser vehicle) was the first teaching of the Buddha, emphasizing the end of suffering through one's own efforts—taming the ongoing chatter of the mind. It emphasizes internalizing the understanding of impermanence and nonattachment. One image of this teaching is the mother fish showing her babies the big fat worm on the hook and telling them of the great importance of nonattachment. In our own lives, we suffer every time we allow ourselves to get hooked. The Eightfold Path provides suggestions including ideas of right livelihood, right view, and right intention to avoid the hook. Of course, the biggest hook of all is our precious story of who we think we are. But that, too, is impermanent. Pema Chödrön teaches that the ego lives in a world where one is always getting hooked by one's negative emotions. This is a kind of "homeland security" of the ego, where my enemies are the source of all my pain.

Mahayana Buddhism (the so-called Greater Vehicle) assumes that, through meditation, you have found a way of stopping the chatter of the mind and the grasping and attachment of the ego. It comprises mind training through two great ways of being in the world. The first is the teaching that nothing is happening anywhere, except for the meaning we give to it. If someone recklessly and dangerously cuts us off on the freeway, it has nothing to do with us. Drive carefully, but don't get hooked by anger. After you have internalized this critically important idea of *sunyata* (that nothing is actually happening), you will begin to see the tremendous amount of suffering that people experience due entirely to the meaning that they attach to events they experience, which hooks them on a negative emotion. With this insight, you can begin to walk on the compassionate path of the bodhisattva, the person who has devoted his or her life to being clear of mind and truly helpful. This is the path of emptiness and compassion. His Holiness the Dalai Lama writes that the wisdom of emptiness and impermanence is inseparable from the compassion of altruism and love.

Finally, *Vajrayana Dzogchen* Buddhism (the great perfection) is the fast track to freedom, liberation, and spaciousness—after you have successfully followed the first two of taming and training. Its teaching is that our experience is profoundly clouded by our conditioning from childhood onward (and perhaps by past lives as well). Everything we experience is passed through our complex and twisted mental filters of fear, judgment, and resentment. The result of clearing away that conditioning is called naked awareness. The great sage Padmasambhava taught that we reach self-liberation through seeing with naked awareness. He wrote a book in the eighth century describing this inspiring path. It is our ego, surrounding us like a shell, that prevents us from experiencing spaciousness, which is our true nature. Since this nature is nonlocal—filling all of space and time—it should be no more surprising, as Voltaire said, "to be born twice than to be born once."

What Survives?

Does any evidence encourage us to believe that we mortals may be able to, as Jesus said, "lay down my life, and take it up again" (John 10:18)? In other words, does anything survive after our bodily death? The answer is yes, an answer provided by the monumental work of psychiatrist Ian Stevenson at the University of Virginia Medical School. Since 1960, Stevenson has been investigating cases in which children, usually three to five years old, begin relating memories of an earlier life to their parents. In his first book, *Twenty Cases Suggestive of Reincarnation*, these children often provided detailed memories of their "previous" wives, husbands, children, and houses. Frequently, they had graphic memories of how they died, in some cases providing information about who killed them.[1] Although the majority of these children with memories and abilities from a previous life live in Asian countries where reincarnation is a common belief, Stevenson has published more than 80 papers in recent years showing memories in children from European and North American families as well.

In the most valuable of Stevenson's cases, the children's previous families were unknown to the children's present parents and lived far away in distant cities or villages. In an important subclass of cases, these young children demonstrated surprising skills and information, such as relating memories in a language different from that spoken by their parents. In one case, a young person from India spoke Bengali in a family that spoke Tamil. In another, a child skillfully played a musical instrument he had never seen before.

To verify these remarkable claims, Stevenson or his associates interviewed both the child's family members and the supposed previous distant family, ideally before the two families met. When the families were united, profound emotions often followed. For example, one five-year-old boy greeted his ostensible former wife and children, showing the emotions appropriate for an adult and remarkable in a little boy. In many cases, the child was able to name many of the former family members and friends. Occasionally, the child was able to locate money hidden in the house, frequently to the embarrassment of surviving family members.

These previous life memories are not necessarily evidence of reincarnation. Rather, they present additional data for the idea that *something nonphysical* does survive our death—be it our thoughts, memories, intentions, or emotional connections. These aspects of our nonlocal consciousness may endure in our world of space and time long after our bodies have returned to ashes and dust.

Stevenson's most recent investigations are even more bizarre than those involving recalled memories. In these cases, children with memories of a past life also have birthmarks or physical deformities that correspond to injuries received in the remembered previous lives. In his book *Where Reincarnation and Biology Intersect*, Stevenson shows photos of children and adults who have physical deformities, corresponding to medical reports and X-rays of the person whom the child remembered as a previous incarnation.[2] In all his studies, however, Stevenson has found that the children eventually forget their memories from ostensible previous lives, usually by the time they reach the age of eight or ten.[3]

Before we are overwhelmed with the idea of "born-again souls," we would be wise to define reincarnation by using what researchers *observe,* in order to separate it from the various religious belief systems that lay claim to it. Robert Almeder, professor of philosophy at Georgia State University, minimally defined the term in the *Journal of Scientific Exploration:*

> There is something essential to some human personalities . . . which we cannot possibly construe solely in terms of either brain states, . . . or biological properties caused by the brain. . . . [F]urther, after biological death, this nonreducible biological trait sometimes persists for some time, in some way, in some place, existing independently of the person's former brain and body. Moreover, after some time, some of these irreducible essential traits of human personality . . . come to reside in other human bodies, either some time during the gestation period, at birth, or shortly after birth.[4]

The childhood appearance of memories, birthmarks, and deformities related to a previous life is consistent with the Eastern belief in the law of karma—the law of cause and effect, or action and reaction. Eastern spiritual philosophies also teach that these memories of past desires and attachments, called *skandhas* in Sanskrit, represent a critically important opportunity for us to learn compassion and gain wisdom as we move from one lifetime to another. It should be pointed out that Nagarjuna did not particularly subscribe to the law of karma. Although scholars have different opinions, it appears that Nagarjuna felt that karma was not an objective law of nature, but rather a subjective projection of the mind. Since karma lacks its own being, it therefore could not be a substantial entity.

Others have hypothesized that memories and emotions may

be imbedded in our cells or organs and that this information can be accessed by the brain of a transplanted organ recipient. Neurobiologist Candace Pert says that the mind is not just in the brain. The neuropeptides of the body, the "biochemicals of emotion," are the messengers for the body-mind, and they are found in the brain as well as the muscles, glands, organs, and so-called enteric brain of the gastrointestinal system. This leads to the hypothesis that the memories and emotions imbedded in our cells or organs contain information that can be accessed by the brain of a transplanted organ recipient.

Knowing that we have a biomolecular basis for emotions, the question then is "How do emotions arise?" Pert suggests that awareness can transform matter by some kind of signal conveyed over time that occurs simultaneously in the nonmaterial and physical substrates of the body. This bidirectional body-mind connection is an example of what Nagarjuna called dependent coarising and also exemplifies the nonlocality of physics. In other words, thoughts trigger biochemical activity that affects the physical body. This is the basis of psychoneuroimmunology. Pert also asks, could the chakras—the seven energy centers of the body—have anything to do with this signal? She discovered that the highest concentration of neuropeptides in the body corresponds with the location of the chakras.[5]

Cellular biologist Bruce Lipton's research on the human immune system has led him to insights on the molecular basis of perceptions and behavior. He says our world and experience are created by our thoughts and beliefs. According to Lipton, individual cells living in a community such as our body must follow a single collective voice or the community would cease. When we extend this community concept throughout our body, or scale upward, we see the importance of how our consciousness in each of its body parts is nested in a *sangha,* a community of spiritual practice. Humanity is destined for a sangha relationship on all levels, putting the parts together instead of ripping them apart, to achieve a totality of life experience. The collective voice controlling the community's expression represents the sum of the perceptions of each single cell. So we are not just a single body, but a *community of intercommunicating single cells.* Likewise, we could think of humanity as a body composed of millions of intercommunicating individuals. And our *sangha,* community, may also cease if we cannot hear the collective voice that is found through the compassion and love that lead to the unconditioned naked awareness available to each and every one of us. Thus the oneness and unity of humanity become increasingly apparent.

We believe that the transfer of memory need not depend on the cell at all, because our minds are nonlocal—*not located inside our brains or bodies.* According to biochemist and author Rupert Sheldrake, "Our minds are more like television sets than video recorders; a television tunes in to transmissions, but it doesn't store them."[6] We agree with author Dr. Larry Dossey's idea that some aspect of an organ donor's consciousness is fundamentally united with the consciousness of the recipient and that receiving the donor's heart somehow intensifies a mental connection that was already present. Just such a case is described in Clare Sylvia's remarkable book *A Change of Heart,* in which a refined New England woman received the heart of an 18-year-old motorcyclist. She later established psychic contact with her donor during her dreams[7] and developed his cravings for beer and Chicken McNuggets.

In the end, philosopher Stephen Braude concludes that the "crushing burden of complexity" of all other explanations leads him to decide in favor of the proposition that some aspect of awareness or personality does indeed survive. And it's *not* just some kind of "super-psi"—a combination of particularly outstanding telepathy combined with clairvoyance—which would allow a medium to know everything about a deceased person.[8]

The important thread running through all these examples is that awareness persists and that our minds are *powerful and nonlocal.* And above all, we are more than just a body. Our memories and our present thoughts affect the thoughts and experiences of ourselves and others in the future. Our memories, emotions, and intentions create information that can be accessed in nonordinary states of awareness, such as dreams and remote viewing.

We are now seeing a whole new concept of mind emerge. We can think of mind as the biological mechanism through which consciousness is managed, or we can think of mind as being part of a global consciousness interaction. The real ramification of this is the sudden recognition of the mutual coarising of the mind and consciousness—what neurophysiologist Karl Pribram calls the holographic mind. Awareness and consciousness are distributed throughout the brain rather than localized in individual parts. The holographic mind presents the exciting possibility that human beings can share in unique transcendental experiences that can usher in an expanded understanding of consciousness. It exists as the ultimate vehicle through which we can momentarily experience a kind of universal Oneness. As Nagarjuna taught, we can experience that ultimate reality called naked awareness. This capacity is incompatible with Newtonian determinism and scientific reductionism, but it is compatible with quantum emergence and the new physics of consciousness.

One of the authors (Hurtak) calls humanity a "living biotransducer."[9] The brain functions as a transducer, bringing psychic signals into our awareness. The holographic mind supports the profound ancient concept that the human race is ultimately to be in association with what some call the Divine or Universal Mind as its source of identity. In the development of the holographic mind, however, one must first address the problem of dualistic thinking and language. Only then can the mind address this collective consciousness.

The existence of mystical phenomena has led many contemporary researchers to state that universal consciousness may be a kind of nonlocal mind. Albert Einstein hated the idea of nonlocality, which contradicted local and mechanistic assumptions of classical physics. Einstein introduced the idea of "hidden variables" to explain how quantum mechanical descriptions of physical reality are not complete. The hidden variable theory stated that underlying the level of indeterminacy of quantum mechanics is an *objective foundation*, whereby distant events are assumed to have no effect on local events. This is a counterproposal to quantum entanglement, which Einstein disparaged as a "spooky connection at a distance." Although Einstein never accepted the idea of nonlocality and quantum entanglement, Schrödinger, David Bohm, and J. S. Bell, along with most contemporary physicists, embraced the idea that we can no longer view objects as existing independently.

In fact, Bell's inequality theorem on nonlocality is considered one of the most profound in science, contributing to research on the nature of consciousness. We are encouraged to revise our concept of local reality consisting of entities separate from each other. Once again, we recall Nagarjuna's teaching that no entity exists independently, that all entities mutually co-arise, which is also descriptive of nonlocality.

Sir John Eccles, Nobel laureate, believes that the nature of human consciousness will probably never be explained by science and "can be sufficiently explained only by recourse to some supernatural origin as well." In *Facing Reality,* Eccles maintains that the mind routinely exerts a true psychokinetic influence on one's own brain through "cognitive caresses" of the synapses of cortical neurons.[10] For all practical purposes, we could view our own nonphysical thoughts as the agency that allows us to extend an arm, by interacting with our own muscles through psychokinesis. Eccles's idea is harmonious with Karl Pribram's model of the holographic brain. For the average person, it is impossible to dissect out, or locate, the place from which the desire to move your arm or leg originates. What is surprising, however, is the idea that we can affect or consider healing *someone else's* body with our thoughts.

Our body-mind is a remarkable instrument attuned to interact and participate with collective consciousness. We all can appreciate that studies in both physics and consciousness have revealed more intricate interconnections than we once dreamed possible.

Spiritual Implication of Our Nonlocal Mind

The nondual, nonlocal Mahayanists (Middle Way Buddhists) looked kindly upon the religious needs of ordinary people and, in addition, they had much to say about the higher stages of the path and, in particular, about the transcendental knowledge and intuition of the ultimate or unconditioned awareness. The new understanding they sought to create was Universal—absorbing both relative and ultimate realities, the ordinary and the pristine—free of conditioning. Such people exist without plurality of object, without departure into division. This is similar to Schrödinger's view that "conscious is a singular that has no plural." These people have discovered that who they are is pure or unbounded awareness. They are not a body, but rather awareness residing for a time as a body. And some aspect of that awareness survives bodily death.

Our ego and our story are among the principal sources of all our suffering and block our path to conscious awareness. When we realize that we are pure awareness, we can finally begin to get rid of our protective and defensive ego, which is the warehouse of our story of who we *think* we are. Thus we begin to experience what the New Testament calls the "kingdom of God"—the experience of who we are as spacious beings, here and everywhere. Then we can begin to drop our ego-created story. When we are able to experience that nothing can separate us from our divine nature, then suddenly there is nothing to fear. And we can finally trade in all our fear, resentment, and judgment for gratitude, peace, and love. This is a choice that can be made any morning, as a way to start your day. The experience of nonseparation is the gift of the nondual ontology. It is the central teaching of this book.

Namkhai Norbu is a contemporary Dzogchen master living in Italy. Of his many books, one of the most accessible and inspiring is *The Mirror: Advice on the Presence of Awareness*. He tries—through direct transmission—to propel the reader out of conditioned awareness, into naked awareness, and thus to experience timeless existence. Freedom and spaciousness are the objectives. He writes:

> Dzogchen doesn't ask you to change your religion, philosophy, or ideology, nor become something other than what you are. It only asks you to observe yourself, and to discover the "cage" you have built with your conditioning and limits. And it teaches you how to get out of the cage, without creating another one, in order to become a free, autonomous person.[11]

The message of *The Mirror,* as in all Dzogchen teachings, is one of crystal clarity and purity. It is critically important for each of us to remember and remain aware that we are the mirror—not all the chaotic things that are reflected in it. Norbu specifically says, "You are the mirror, not the reflection."

Longchenpa is a great Dzogchen master who gives us advice in his inspiring book *The Jewel Ship,* which is as powerful today as when it was written in the twelfth century.[12] He describes the "five passions of conditioned existence," which define the all too familiar walls of the cage from which Norbu is also helping us to free ourselves. They define the nature of our personal story, or what the Buddhists refer to as the ego or the small self. The small self is contrasted with the Self that is our divine nature in touch with the *darmakaya* or nonlocal awareness that many call God. Longchenpa doesn't want us to fixate on these hindrances to freedom, just notice them and let them go. The five passions to be released are:

• Lust—not to be confused with love, nor allowed to run your life.
• Anger—always in service to the small self or ego: "They're not doing it my way."
• Arrogance—puffed up with infinite nothingness: the tragic confusion of your self with your story.
• Jealousy—you already have within you limitless love and everything else you could possibly want.
• Stupidity—you know the truth and choose differently.

As with Christianity's seven deadly sins (pride, envy, gluttony, lust, anger, greed, sloth), each of us will have our own personal favorite. Longchenpa goes on to tell us: "There will never be freedom, for there never has been bondage. . . . There is only

self-knowing awareness, the blissful place of rest extending infi-
nitely as the supremely spacious state of spontaneous equalness
[spontaneity]."[13] This is our goal.

Your Story

In writing of the passions in which we cage ourselves, we
can't help thinking again of our beloved and enigmatic Marilyn
Monroe. Everybody loved Marilyn Monroe. She had money,
beauty, fame, security, means of expression, and great recognition. Since these are things that we all seek and she had them in
abundance, why did she keep trying to kill herself—and possibly
eventually succeed (by accident)?

At this point in the chapter, we all know the answer. She created "Marilyn Monroe," as a supreme comedic accomplishment.
Although many moviegoers considered her to be no more than
a blonde tart, there were numerous serious-minded critics who
viewed her as a serious actress. Lee Strasberg of the Actors'
Studio and her playwright husband, Arthur Miller, both thought
she was one of the great actresses of the century. Jean-Paul Sartre
said that she was the greatest actress alive. Her tragedy is that she
came to believe that her posters, her made-up *persona* of "the
girl," and her business card represented who she was, rather
than just being her story. One of her many tragedies was that at
a time when she was the most profitable and famous star in
Hollywood, Fox was paying her only ten percent of what other
actors on the set with her were receiving. It's worth thinking
about how that could happen. Miller writes of his late wife, "the
simple fact, terrible and lethal, was that no space whatever
existed between herself and the star. *She was 'Marilyn Monroe,'
and that was what was killing her.*" [emphasis added] Constant

waiting for applause is enough to turn a person inside out. We must give up waiting for applause, waiting for anything.

Marilyn Monroe was not alone. Many of our most beloved and immensely popular superstars pay a great price for their incandescent fame. By their constant exposure to money, power, and huge audiences of manic and adoring fans, these performers open themselves to having their true self sucked right out of their body, and having it replaced by a false self projected upon them by their fans. Janis Joplin, Jim Morrison (of The Doors), Jimi Hendrix, and Elvis Presley, "the King," all died young as a result of self-inflicted drug overdoses. These Dionysian characters with their pink Cadillacs allowed themselves to be psychically torn apart by the fans, just as the ecstatic followers (*meneads*) of the mythic Dionysius would tear animals apart and devour their raw flesh as part of their frenzy. The Beatles appear to have escaped this fate for several important reasons. They had devoted wives or girlfriends who kept them grounded, and they eventually found mind-quieting meditation and a spiritual teacher. Their passionate pro-peace, anti-war beliefs gave their lives meaning and focus—their lives were "about something" outside of themselves and the ringing telephone. Also, it is interesting to point out that their drug of choice was LSD, which is an entheogen, fostering feelings of spaciousness and even the divine, whereas barbiturates, amphetamines, and alcohol contract a person's experience, often leading to a mental implosion.

In the same way, engineers at Lockheed (where I, Targ, worked for a decade) often work there for a lifetime—30 or more years. Frequently, when they retire, they live a shockingly short time—two or three years. In my calculation, they die significantly sooner than actuarially predicted, by odds of 20 to one. Pretty scary for those of us who worked there. I believe the reason for the premature death is that their business card or story card says these men are a "Lockheed (or Boeing) engineer." They have lost their identity, and losing their life isn't far behind. Actuarially, a man who lives to be 65 has avoided the perils of war, car crashes, hunting accidents, and the other events that shorten men's lives. Such a person would normally be expected to live into their eighties (79 is the mean). When they retire, after a lifetime of service, they are suddenly "nothing." One of my good friends at Lockheed, who was the head of marketing, bought a little house in the country. He told us he wanted to "get out of the pressure cooker while he still had a chance to smell the flowers." He had a fatal heart attack one week after his retirement party. To my mind, this shows the very serious penalty one pays for believing his or her story. As Miller observed, believing your story is lethal.

Survival of Bodily Death

The great English classicist F. W. H. Myers was one of the founders of the Society for Psychical Research in 1882. In his encyclopedic book *Human Personality and Its Survival of Bodily Death,* he gives many extraordinary examples of how some recognizable portion of the personality actually survives death.[14] Then after his own death, he gave strong evidence of his own survival by appearing in the consciousness of several mediums in different countries and by providing them with unique personal information. These communications led to a ten-year investigation into what became known as the *cross-correspondence case.* This confirms Ian Stevenson's cases of reincarnation, in *Children Who Remember Previous Lives,* which convincingly demonstrate that some of these personalities actually reappear in bodily form, with clear memories of previous lives.

According to Robert Almeder, "We now have, for the first time in the history of our species, compelling empirical evidence for belief in some form of personal survival after death."[15] Or again, as Voltaire said, "It is no more surprising to be born twice than to be born once." Most of us, although we may avoid asking it aloud, at one time or another wonder, "Do we live out our lives and then vanish like a bubble, leaving not a trace?" This enduring question is directly related to our search for meaning and our passion to discover who we really are.

Here, we have described the many ways in which our conscious selves can experience oneness with the infinite nonlocal universe. It has been our intention to present not only philosophy, but also research data that confirm nonlocal experience of life. And we further suggest that a nonconscious part of ourselves has a similar connection—a part, as you are doubtless aware, that is often called our spirit or soul.

My (Targ's) teacher Gangaji, in the nondual *advaita vedanta* tradition of Ramana Maharshi, has written an exquisite little book called *Freedom and Resolve,* describing the path of self-inquiry and the life-and-death issue of discovering who we are. In a chapter called "The Story of 'Me,'" she presents the inescapable importance of recognizing our story for what it is, and then—in spite of what our ego says—surrendering it. She writes:

> The first challenge is to recognize that you are telling a story. Then the challenge is in having the willingness to die, and in that, the willingness to be nothing at all. Then, this that we have called Self or Truth or God is revealed to be that very same no-thing at all. You recognize yourself as that no-thing [just timeless awareness].[16]

Notes

1. Ian Stevenson, *Twenty Cases Suggestive of Reincarnation,* New York: American Society for Psychical Research, 1966; *European Cases of the Reincarnation Type,* Jefferson, NC: McFarland, 2003.

2. Ian Stevenson, *Where Reincarnation and Biology Intersect,* Westport, CT: Praeger, 1997.

3. Ian Stevenson, *Children Who Remember Previous Lives,* Charlottesville, VA: University Press of Virginia, 1987.

4. R. Almeder, "A critique of arguments offered against reincarnation," *Journal of Scientific Exploration* 11:4 (1997).

5. Candace Pert, *Molecules of Emotion: The Science behind Mind-Body Medicine,* New York: Scribner, 1999.

6. Rupert Sheldrake, in Claire Sylvia, *A Change of Heart,* New York: Little Brown, 1997.

7. Claire Sylvia, *A Change of Heart,* New York: Little Brown, 1997.

8. Stephen E. Braude, *Immortal Remains: The Evidence for Life after Death,* Lanham, MD: Rowman and Littlefield, 2003.

9. J. J. Hurtak, "The meaning to life in theories of language and biology," in *Future History,* Series 3, vol. 3, Los Gatos, CA: Academy for Future Science, 2000, p. 10.

10. John Eccles, *Facing Reality,* New York: Springer-Verlag, 1970.

11. Namkhai Norbu, *The Mirror: Advice on the Presence of Awareness,* Barrytown, NY: Barrytown, 1996.

12. Longchenpa, "The Jewel Ship," in *You Are the Eyes of the World,* Ithaca, NY: Snow Lion Publications, 2000.

13. Longchen Rabjam (Longchenpa), *The Precious Treasury of the Basic Space of Phenomena,* Junction City, CA: Podma Publishing, 2001. This remarkable book is a powerful "transmission" all by itself.

14. F. W. H. Myers, *Human Personality and Its Survival of Bodily Death,* Charlottesville, VA: Hampton Roads, 2001 (originally published 1903).

15. Robert F. Almeder, *Death and Personal Survival: The Evidence for Life after Death,* Lanham, MD: Rowman and Littlefield, 1992.

16. Gangaji, *Freedom and Resolve: The Living Edge of Surrender,* Novato, CA: Gangaji Foundation, 1999.

10

Release from Suffering: A Path to Integration

You are beyond all obstacles: self-arising pristine awareness just is.

—Longchenpa

A Guide to Fearless Living

Defending Your Life is a remarkably intelligent Hollywood film about the importance of learning to live your life without fear. The premise is that we all live multiple lives on Earth, and each time we die, we go to Judgment City (which looks like an upscale suburban mall), where we are evaluated by judges. It isn't the traditional "heaven or hell" decision. Instead, if we have finally overcome fear, we move on to something better. If not, we are thrown back to Earth, where we must lead yet another life and continue this karmic cycle until we have demonstrated that we have discovered fearless living. The implication is that if you *don't* get it, they will eventually throw you out! For Daniel (Albert Brooks) this is a touching situation, because he is a somewhat paranoid person. It is further complicated by his meeting beautiful and fearless Julia (Meryl Streep), who no doubt will move forward. Brooks has been bullied all his life. And even on his last day in purgatory, he is afraid to express his love for the fetching Julia, who is the kind of person who runs into a burning building to save her pet cat. (In spite of the daunting setup, this morality play does have a happy ending.)

Discovering the Truth

The Aristotelian mind-world dichotomy has fractured human consciousness. We can never discover our true nature through a *purely physical* model of reality—which is not in itself wrong; it is simply not comprehensive enough. It's as though we can't see the forest for the trees. Obsessively examining the parts, we ignore the whole, which includes both relative truth and ultimate truth. For the highest good of all, we need a holistic epistemology uniting knowledge of the mechanisms of physical reality with the subjective experience of human consciousness.

Aldous Huxley proclaimed that the mind has to be "funneled through the reducing valve of the brain and the nervous system. What comes out at the other end is a measly trickle" of consciousness.[1] We experience reality through a filter called conditioned awareness, which is the source of our particular version of the truth. It is this conditioned awareness that brings about disharmony (dis-ease) and obscures the true purpose of human existence. It's important to recognize that every event that occurs in our lives will contain different truths. Suffering occurs when we neglect the multiple truths that comprise reality. So we embrace the nondual view of reality, which integrates holistic and analytic knowledge.

In many Eastern traditions, the body is considered a microcosm of the universe, with fields of energy considered vibrational centers (chakras) communicating with fields of energy both outside and inside the body. For example, in Taoist Chinese systems of acupuncture, the energy body is a pattern of acupuncture points on meridians, energy currents that extend to the cosmos, through which energy can be transmitted or communicated.[2]

In the biblical tradition, the Psalms (*Tehillim*, "Praises") speak of our connection with the Divine and our ability to transcend boundaries of the isolated self. Some 2,500 years ago, King David wrote:

If I should ascend, there you would be; and if I should spread out my couch in Sheol, look! You would be there. Were I to take the wings of the dawn, that I might reside in the most remote sea, there also your own hand would lead me, and your right hand would lay hold of me . . . (Ps. 139:8–10).

Shamans in Africa, the Pacific, and South America, Christian mystics, and Buddhist and Hindu sages have all understood that we are multidimensional beings connected to the entire universe. Research in physics and parapsychology shows that physical reality is nonlocal, undivided wholeness. Quantum mechanical models provide a solution to the observer-observed problem. We know without a doubt that there is some kind of connection between mind and matter, even if we don't perfectly understand what it is. But in the end, we as individuals are responsible for extending ourselves into the realization of our multidimensional nature inherent in human consciousness. If we are to break through to naked awareness, we need a process that accepts consciousness as inseparable from the material world. Einstein said:

> A human being is part of the whole. Our task is to free ourselves from the prison [of the illusion of separation] through an ever widening circle of compassion to embrace all living creatures and the whole of nature in its beauty.[3]

So how do we break out of the mind-matter prison of illusion? We begin with our willingness to synthesize the rational and mystical and to share our experiences on the path of expanded awareness and self-realization in the service of all creation. It is important to understand that there is really no contradiction between the world of the scientist and the world of the mystic because both deal entirely with experience rather than belief. Both deal with data derived from experience rather than dogma. Expanded awareness is available to all humanity. One needn't be a yogi or ascetic. One of the authors (Hurtak) describes this in *The Book of Knowledge: The Keys of Enoch®,* calling it a movement into more creative levels of the human-God partnership.[4]

When physical reality and sacred space are undivided, body, mind, and spirit move into spaciousness and timeless awareness, where we give up judgment and experience our inherent loving nature, rejuvenation, and healing. The Kabbalists symbolized this integration of body-mind-spirit through the Tree of Life. Using this metaphor, we begin with the world as our kingdom *(Malkuth)*, then elevate our awareness through the balance of Wisdom *(Chokmah)* and Understanding *(Binah)*, thus balancing peace with power and work with joy. Finally, we reach divine unfolding represented by the Crown *(Kether)* of Love and mastery over our chaotic world. Kether is the jumping-off point for *Ain Soph*, which is our experience of timeless awareness or eternity. At this level of integration, we achieve full consciousness in the ongoing nature of the cosmos. The point of all this is that the structure of the kabbalistic Tree of Life is not only a description of consciousness, but when internalized in meditation, can be a vehicle of transformation of consciousness.

I (Hurtak) wrote in 1973, "Man must consider himself as part of a larger field of intelligence operating as part of these [greater] interrelationships. He can break the matter-energy construct through certain forms of mind expansion."[5] The primary objective—the supreme accomplishment of all life and education—is the full awakening of human consciousness and the complete restoration of humanity into wholeness of being.

In the Christian tradition, the apostle Paul tells us to "let Christ dwell in your hearts" in order to grasp mentally "the breadth and length and height and depth" that surpasses knowledge (Eph. 3:17, 18). The putting on of this "mind of Christ" is the invitation to unconditional love. It is the realization of the mind that is not earthbound or self-centered, but is of service to the All at all times and under all conditions. One begins awakening oneself through the simple process of altering consciousness—perhaps to experience the Divine Presence, which is who we are.

An Outline of Suggested Practice

What is the groundwork for this process that primarily is undoing the ego? It is revealed in five basic principles in line with the historical teachings of the perennial philosophy.

First—We are all one in consciousness. You become willing to embrace an *integrative ontology* that recognizes the unity of all—no separation or judgment of others. Nagarjuna provided his tetralemma as a way to prove his doctrine of dependent arising and emptiness, to enable us to let go fearlessly of the attachment to physical reality, which fosters division of mind and cosmos. It is important to know that essentially *nothing is happening*, except in your mind. You may choose an exemplary teacher such as Nagarjuna, the Buddha, or Jesus to guide you in the process of creative renewal. Or you can find a peaceful, openhearted teacher in your own neighborhood.

Second—Quiet the ongoing mental chatter. You allow yourself time for *daily self-reflection*—prayer, meditation, forgiveness, and gratitude. The toning and pacifying effects of meditation on brain waves, blood pressure, and heart rate have been well documented over the past decades in many scientific research laboratories, and particularly in the work of Dr. Herbert Benson at Harvard University Medical School.[6] There are many ways to release our old mind-set. I (Hurtak), in collaboration with musicians and Howard Wills, who specializes in both local and distant healing, have created a series of healing affirmations that can be a powerful healing tool for those who are open to the release of the old mind and the adopting of the new. Nagarjuna tells us to change our thought perspective. One of the ways to do this is through the process of forgiveness and emptying your mental backpack of smelly old resentments, for you soon realize that you must remove yourself from the hostilities and troubling thought forms that link you with past memories and inhibit your compassion and unconditional love for all beings.

One of Wills's successful positive affirmations is as follows:[7]

I bless this day and give thanks for my life
I forgive completely all people who have hurt me
I ask all people I have hurt to please forgive me

I apologize to myself
For my wrongs to myself and my wrongs to others

I apologize for all my hurts or wrongs to all life forms

With this release, freedom, peace, power, and new life,
I bless all creation in the entire universe
And I fill the entire universe with my love
I love and bless the earth, all life, and all humanity
I love, bless, and respect the visible and the invisible
I rejoice and give thanks for my new life, power, and health,
I give complete blessing and love to all life, always.

As with all affirmations and the practice of forgiveness, it is the daily practice of these activities that strengthens their effectiveness as keys for the release of *dis-ease*. We're not, however, required to sit in the lotus position in a mountain retreat for hours on end, though it wouldn't hurt. As little as five or ten minutes of meditation at a time—every day—is beneficial and can be managed even while at work, on public transportation, anywhere you can sit quietly and breathe.

Third—Oneness leads to the *practice of compassion.* You continue to study and work on understanding yourself and others. As you begin to change your perspective of seeing everything as "I" to seeing "we" or "us," then you can understand how and why you react as you do. You begin to see things from other perspectives. Continuing practice develops compassion, allowing you to open inner doors of perception, thereby experiencing unity. This unitive experience is one of the things that gives meaning to your life. It is also a good time to investigate and surrender much of the story of who you think you are.

Fourth—Having experienced the flow of loving awareness, share that experience. *Share in fellowship with others* in your spiritual community (revered by Buddhists as the *sangha*); be an active participant while maintaining the guiding principles within yourself. You must go beyond the individual personality and ego to experience unity and fellowship without judgment or condemnation. We cannot overstate the importance of participating in some sort of spiritual sharing community. Humanity's true nature is not individualistic but finds its real essence in working and sharing in a community of spirit that allows the fullness of who we are to shine forth. The perennial philosophy teaches that after we have had a unitive experience of oneness, or the Divine, we want to share that experience. "I am here to be truly helpful" *(A Course in Miracles).*

Fifth—Surrender and give up negativity and judgment of others. You must *reflect positive thinking,* which brings personal healing. You become a problem-solver, rather than residing in negativity. This is a reflection of your ability to interact more meaningfully and closely with others. In this way, you can work toward greater compassion, fellowship, and community of spirit, where collective affirmations are made and where healing can take place. In essence, Earth cannot be changed for the better unless the consciousness of each individual is changed. You can pledge to work for such transformation, within yourself and your community, by taking time to experience the flow of loving awareness which is your true nature—what the apostle Paul called the peace beyond human understanding (Phil. 4:7). And in line with this limitless peace, you will find a way to simplify your life as the Buddhists teach: empty, empty, happy, happy.

Living with Timeless Awareness

Life takes on a whole new meaning when we realize that our experience need not be formed exclusively by our five senses, but is also formed of consciousness. We begin to live in the eternity of the moment, no longer bounded by space and time. Our focus is different. We become present and create a more spacious reality, rather than being rueful of the past and fearful of the future. We stop being a small self with jealousies and fears, wanting to grab, hold, and accumulate. We are instead guided beyond our self-centered fears into new realms where we experience oceanic connection with nature and humanity. We transcend the boundaries of self. This nondual spacious awareness ultimately leads us to helpfulness, compassion, and service.

Our life in this world is not an illusion, and we have an opportunity to exercise our free will. This significantly implies being responsible for whatever we do and experience. A problem arises when we, as eternal beings, lose the awareness of our true nature and begin to *identify ourselves* with material, transient forms such as our bodies, possessions, or feelings. For the most part, the physical universe is the only dimension of reality humanity senses. And that is why Nagarjuna encourages us to go beyond our two-valued logic system to discover our true nature and integrate our emergent spirituality with the ever-unfolding Cosmos.

Let's ask ourselves: What are we doing on planet Earth and what is our ultimate purpose? We have been taught that Nature is here to be tamed and that her incredible array of complex systems is merely the result of accidental happenings. But we will discover that we are divine beings who only need to wake up to a new cartography of consciousness that makes use of the power of Love that is all around and within us. To awaken, we need to transcend the materialistic scripting that many of us have inherited from both philosophical and scientific rationalism. Here we realize that the real purpose of life is to be one with the greater universal consciousness, which is in and of all things, and to help others share in this profound unitive experience. To experience this spaciousness is to experience the glory of the suns and stars within our consciousness.

Gerard Manley Hopkins writes in his poem "Pied Beauty": "Glory be to God for dappled things." Those who remain asleep go from task to task unsurprised by the infinite beauty of transient things. Enlightened beings cherish their world; they live and work and love. Remaining in three-dimensional enslavement means living in a restricted space as opposed to experiencing the divine harmony of the Whole. Although the physical body starts as a single cell that grows into an enclosed self-regulated system of trillions of cells, this physical part comes and goes. Our mind and consciousness are never limited, so why should we limit ourselves while we are here?

More to the point, how can we end suffering? Physical pain is not always optional, but suffering from ignorance is. Whether in ignorance or with knowledge, each human being is responsible for the consequences of his or her thoughts, words, and deeds. We can choose to suffer or we can choose to release ourselves from our limitations through greater knowledge of the universe and of who we really are. The release is not always just a mental release, it sometimes comes by changes in the physical circumstances of our life. We may need to change on all levels, in order to initiate our change of mental reality. For most, it is as easy as instituting a daily practice of meditation or affirmations, or a new mode of thinking and perceiving others. Some more extreme situations might require, however, a change of associations, work, or physical locations in order to free ourselves from whatever is limiting us.

Cogito, ergo sum—*"I think therefore I am"* is the *"I am"* construct of being. As we expand this view of ourselves into a greater "we," we ultimately become unified with the flow of loving awareness and become synergistic with all life as cocreator. By our expanded effort, we discover the "infinite" and the "plane of the Absolute that knows only truth" *(ritam bhara pragyam)*. We do this not by straining to escape from the finite, but by a complete acceptance of the limitlessness of ourselves. And therefore we arrive at an understanding of the immemorial experience as found in the Bible (Exod 3:14)—the experience of the "I AM THAT I AM" or "I WILL BECOME WHAT I WILL BECOME." Many have never actually understood the meaning of these words. The incredible truth that religion calls the vision of God is found in giving up any belief in *the idea of God as a static reality of personhood.* The relativist often fails to reach this point because he or she does not follow this line of thought consistently. The discovery of the mystery, the wonder of the greater life is beyond any imagination and comes only through the experience of letting go of the self-centered "I" to be one with the ongoing nature of Life. This is the experience of the mystic that leads to liberation.

Ultimately, we are to go beyond duality, which then gives us the ability to go beyond the individual "I" into the universal "I AM" or we. Here we overcome the dualistic way of splitting humanity into parts or conceptualizing through the world of intellectual ideals as opposed to working open-mindedly with the world of pluralistic realities. Linguistically, nobody speaks of my body becoming consciousness, but simply and powerfully I AM CONSCIOUSNESS. In such spiritual development, the inner "I am" ultimately merges into unity with the divine epiphany, which is transcendent, beyond words as the rapture of the soul. By simply paying attention to here and now, moment by moment, we can begin this process of experiencing the universal consciousness within ourselves.

From a classical standpoint, consciousness has been understood to be the property of the individual or the "I" that is supposed to enable one to know who one is. But this is incorrect. Consciousness is like a current originating in the oceanic collective consciousness and becoming part of the individual. The fuller "I AM" intrinsically has neither definite time nor definite space.

The Ego and I

The "ego-I," however, represents the covering over of one's original naked awareness and is the source of almost all of our suffering. If we think of ourselves as eternal, we are correct. If we see ourselves as individuals only, then we are in illusion because in reality we are always part of the Whole. We have free will and our reconnection to fuller consciousness is never forced on us. We can remain asleep as long as we wish. But under the influence of the ego, our original state of consciousness is covered and eclipsed. Our ego, intellect, and story block us from the experience of eternity, which is timeless and spaceless.

In reality, we are neither independent nor God-forsaken, but are eternally one with the Whole, aware of our collective identity. This makes us, as Nagarjuna asserted, one with Truth and Nature. This nondivided oneness is the meaning of the Love that reconnects us to Truth beyond duality, to one another, and to our inner divinity, which is the flow of loving awareness within. As a practical result, we are able to see everything—even the negative—in the light of this oneness. To experience this is to experience the end of suffering.

We want to clarify the point that oneness doesn't imply loss of our uniqueness as individuals. We do not become like the Borg group-mind of *Star Trek*. Our uniqueness and our personal goals remain even while we are One. We are all unique as an expression of life, and yet it is pointless and self-defeating to be proud, to try to impress others with our uniqueness. All attempts to express "my singularity" on a material level quickly lead to egoic competitions and personal suffering.

Deep psychological healing takes place through cultivating the connected nature of humanity. In the East and among Native Americans, this was historically done in spiritual art and dance, where the circle or mandala—representing the wheel of the world—was manifested in fellowship. The image of the cosmic wheel depicts humans as self-reflecting, microcosmic, and macrocosmic beings finding fulfillment in the experience of our divinity and the sharing of that experience. As Longchenpa would say, we are united in the basic space of phenomena.

As we discover the Eternal, Infinite, and Fullness of bliss *(Ananda)*, we find ourselves living as multidimensional beings in a multidimensional universe not limited by ordinary concepts of space and time. The evidence for this is our direct experience of nonlocal awareness, which allows us to describe and experience distant and future events. We realize we have been significantly unaware of our surroundings and have understood only a mere sliver of reality. But now we begin to feel interconnected as Pure-Being Consciousness—naked awareness. And with this we find that suffering vanishes—no more *maya*. *Maya*, literally "that which I am not," is illusion and false identification. *Maya* begins when we, as eternal beings, identify ourselves with noneternal conditioned awareness, such as our bodies, our feelings, and our accomplishments. It is the identification with something that we are not rather than with spaciousness. The illusion of *maya* always exists, but we get to choose whether or not to be trapped in its illusion.

Seeing ourselves as separate from Nature and Truth is the illusion of *maya*. The rational mind reconstructs its sensory world through dualistic logic. Therefore we suffer. This dualistic logic is what Nagarjuna tried to help us to overcome. In reality, *maya* is nothing but a state of covered consciousness, which brings with it the confusion of identity and identification with ego. It can be transcended by restoring our being into the fuller consciousness of Oneness and timeless awareness.

Duality is a (relative) reality, just as darkness is a relative reality for those who are separated from the light. Mental darkness or spiritual ignorance leads to illusion and false identification, literally. If duality were real, then good and evil would exist. Evil is the self-serving imploding energy of ego—the absence of good—rather than a force of its own. It is empty of meaning except for the meaning we give to it. Likewise, spiritual darkness or ignorance is merely the absence of light or awareness. Ego with its concomitant judgment is the principal reason for spiritual darkness and suffering.

Discovering the Divine

Who or what is obstructing the natural flow of loving awareness? Nothing else but our ego when we forget our true identity as Eternal. When engaged in practices such as remote viewing, as well as spiritual healing, a person no longer is operating solely as a biological organism. We realize we are not defined atomically in terms of particles and waves, but are part of a consciousness outside space-time, participating in a higher-dimensional nonlocal universe. And then we understand Nagarjuna's tetralemma: I am a body; I am not a body; I am both a body and not a body; and I am neither a body nor not a body. This is the true solution to the famous mind-body problem. As a bodily organism, we are finite, mortal, and subject to suffering, but at the same time, we are not a body but a consciousness, living in a multidimensional universe.

What brings about this transcendent state of mind? Surrendering the ego brings about the liberated consciousness of no mind and no expectation. It is known by various names in the East such as *Moksha* (liberation), Qi Gong, Aikido, and Zen. In the Western traditions, it was known to the ancient Greeks as gaining Sophia, the indwelling of feminine higher wisdom or the mothering nature of the universe. In the Kabbalah, the same path to the Divine is called *Shekinah*. As we cultivate our intuitive nature, we enter into this wisdom.

We need to redefine our true nature, which is neither biological nor mythological, but functional and extensional. This expansion of awareness (extending to fill all of space and time) starts by understanding matter as Cosmic energy, manifesting in endless numbers of transient forms. Within our spiritual self-realization, the substructure of microcosm and macrocosm are wedded into Unity. In Western mystical tradition, this can be symbolized in the Tree of Life *(Etz Chaim),* known in the West within kabbalistic literature in which humankind participates with its generative and regenerative process. This new criterion of human nature sees "Man" and "Woman" as a composite of energy embodiments and self-realizations.

If this is our true nature, why do we see ourselves as limited to these bodies and suffer from such a narrow perspective? And if we change our perspective, what happens to us as we emerge into the larger consciousness as an expanded "New Being"? As remote viewing and spiritual healing have shown, we are capable of transcending this time-binding linguistic, psychobiological existence. Remote viewing and spiritual healing are exceptionally well documented in the scientific literature. When we truly realize our inner connection with all life, we cease to suffer from a limited mental perception of life. Understanding our unboundedness, we still value life. This is very important. The three-dimensional realm can nurture our growth, learning, and sharing. It is not a place from which we must leave or physically depart. But as others join us in this expanded awareness, we will emerge into one of the greatest eras of growth our species has ever known, as we pass from an era of individualism to one of global conscious identity. Such passing, as history shows, has always been painful for some and joyful for others. It is shaped by the consequences of admitting the limitations of the traditional paradigms of our view of reality.

We can already see that many are joining in. There are transitions occurring at this time in science, even in the face of resistance to relinquishing concepts once accepted as "standard." Periods of bewilderment often accompany these transitions, as, for instance, the passing from the Ptolemaic to the Copernican view of the cosmos, from Euclidean to non-Euclidean, from Newtonian to non-Newtonian (Einsteinian)—and now from Einsteinian relativity to nonquantum nonlocality. Max Planck, the great German physicist, said that quantum mechanics will be accepted only after the old classical physicists die and are replaced by new ones who have grown up with the new quantum physics.

The End of Duality

Only now, at this late stage of Western civilization, are we beginning to realize how pernicious and retarding the Aristotelian split has been. Einstein and Minkowski have helped us to understand that space and time cannot be split empirically without creating delusional worlds for ourselves. Only since their work have the accomplishments of modern subatomic and undivided space-time physics become possible. In this new physics of consciousness, we are a significant part of the reality we perceive. And we, too, change along with what is observed. It is understood today that you cannot separate the observer from the observed.

Now we are able to entertain the inner wonders of the diversity of life in the greater cosmos. No longer must we live with an artificial split between scientific rationalism and humanistic orientations. What is required is simply our humility and the openness and willingness to accept what is found within us. The New Being we experience is free to live in love, justice, truth, and harmony, leading to the discovery of universal Oneness.

Now we move away from seeing life purely on the basis of dualistic emotional, instinctual relations and logic-based, rational experience. Instead, we are to see life and its interactions in a nonconceptual objective and subjective unity that is Truth.

Finally, the end of suffering is accomplished when we coshape or cocreate *each moment*. Realizing we are not alone, we are never alone. Then the temporary nature of all material things, including our bodies, is no longer seen fearfully. We perceive ourselves in our true identity as eternal awareness.

In truth, time is actually not passing. We live in eternity and the days that pass are a continuum. We live in the eternal present and the only thing that matters is how we live our lives.

In the end, oceanic Love is the purest expression of human free will and human knowing of the Absolute. We are asked in the sacred texts to love all people equally because we are part of divinity—with compassion for each other and concern for all nations.

In conclusion, we have tried to show the need for each one of us to embrace the universal consciousness. Then we can step forward with a holistic perspective of life within and without, unifying science and spirituality. We integrate our contemporary experiences of psychical research and new science with higher states of consciousness that openly support expanded awareness.

With this, we introduce a new, fully conscious being. We recognize and use a fuller understanding of how to open the door of the mind and reconnect with the fuller universal consciousness. We internalize the idea that the key to this door is the understanding that the end of suffering comes when we no longer live our lives protecting and embellishing the story of *me*. We learn to quiet our mind, give up our conditioning, and move into the loving embrace of spacious awareness, which is who we are.

Notes

1. Aldous Huxley, *The Doors of Perception,* San Francisco: Panther Press, 1977.

2. J. J. Hurtak, "Acupuncture and the cycle of birth as viewed in an historic Japanese medical text," *Journal of Alternative and Complementary Medicine* 10:2 (2004).

3. Albert Einstein, *Ideas and Opinions,* New York: Crown, 1954.

4. J. J. Hurtak, *The Book of Knowledge: The Keys of Enoch®,* Los Gatos, CA: Academy for Future Science, 1973.

5. Ibid, 104:39.

6. Herbert Benson, *The Relaxation Response,* New York: William Morrow, 1975.

7. Howard Wills and J. J. Hurtak, *Wings of Healing,* music CD, produced by Academy for Future Science, Los Gatos, CA (www.wings ofhealing.net).

Glossary

AIN SOPH. (Heb.) "Endless." "Infinite." A term frequently used in medieval and postmedieval kabbalistic or philosophic literature to indicate the Unknowable, where *Ain* means "not" and *Soph* means "end," literally "not end," or endless.

ALOBHA. (Sans.) Nonattachment.

ANANDA. (Sans.) "Bliss." In Buddhism, "the fullness of bliss" or "happiness" is a state of mind that is achieved by awakening from the illusions and temptations of the material world.

ARISTOTELIAN LOGIC. A logic of the Greek philosopher Aristotle, emphasizing a dualistic outlook. The search for world structures along the lines of the structural peculiarities of Hellenistic language in which, for example, the use of the word "is" determines doctrine and identity. Through the use of Aristotelian language, higher orders of rationality and adjustment to nondualistic realities were impossible.

ATMAN. (Sans.) The innermost essence of each individual. In some schools of Chinese Buddhism, *atman* equals "soul."

BHUTA-TATHATA. (Sans.) Suchness of existence. Bhuta is substance. Tathata is suchness. Here the immutable is contrasted with form and phenomena of "things."

BINARY. Having two states of possibilities, normally 0 and 1.

BRAHMA. (Sans.) The creator god of the Hindu triad.

BRAHMAN. (Sans.) The ultimate ground of all being in Hinduism.

CONDITIONED AWARENESS. Awareness or a state influenced by previous thinking habits or mind-sets.

DHARMA. (Sans.) (1) The teachings of the Buddha. (2) Phenomena in general.

DHARMAKAYA. (Sans.) (1) The existence of the enlightened body outside of space and time. (2) Reality body with nonlocal awareness.

DRSTIJNANA. (Sans.) "Thought," literally "to view knowledge."

DRSTI-VADA. (Sans.) View, vision, or description. Implies the theory that the subjective perception creates the world as we perceive it and that there are no other objective phenomena apart from what is subjective and perception.

DUKKHA. (Sans.) "Suffering." In the Madhyamika, the basic condition of material and mental life.

DUPLE. Consisting of two or pairs. In logic, means anything that symbolizes two things, propositions, or elements. This can include two levels of meaning or cognitive operations that are superpositioned at the same time.

DZOGCHEN. A form of Tibetan Buddhism renowned for its use of subtle thought and techniques necessary to transcend conditioned awareness and become enlightened, obliterating obstacles without a path.

EIGHTFOLD PATH. The Buddhist concept that is part of the Fourth Noble Truth and details eight activities to be pursued as a way to end suffering and seek enlightenment, including: right understanding, right motives, right speech, right action, right livelihood, right effort, right intellectual activity, and right contemplation.

ETZ CHAIM. (Heb.) "Tree of Life." A philosophical blueprint in mystical or kabbalistic Judaism through which the vehicle of the human body gradually assimilates the divine attributes of the Godhead through finding and cultivating the divine sparks *(sephiroth)* hidden in human nature.

FOUR NOBLE TRUTHS. The doctrines of Buddha: All life is suffering, the cause of suffering is ignorant desire, this desire can be released, the means to this is the Eightfold Path.

FOUR-VALUED LOGIC. A logic of four lemmas used by Nagarjuna

and Madhyamika Buddhist thinkers that allows for the logical reality of going beyond the "excluded middle" and the "excluded ends" in noncontradictory thinking and argument.

GÖDEL'S INCOMPLETENESS THEOREM. A mathematical proof indicating the critical relationship between consistency (2-valued logic) and completeness in all logical systems.

"I AM THAT I AM." In Hebrew, *Ehyeh Asher Ehyeh,* an expression of the proclaimed Name of God uttered to Moses in the experience of Divine manifestation as recorded in the Torah (Exod. 3:14-17) and rendered by some scholars and linguistics as "I Will Be What I Will Be."

JNANAM ADVAYAM. (Sans.) Nondualistic truth or knowledge.

KENOSIS. (Gk.) To "empty out" or renounce divine attributes or higher powers to do the work of a human in acts of charity.

LAW OF NEGATION. Where ~ (~x) = x. This extends to the Law of the Excluded Middle: X OR ~X = TRUE, and also De Morgan's theorem Laws where not (E and F) = (not E) or (not F); or not (E or F) = (not E) and (not F).

LEMMA. (1) Philosophical or mathematical proposition accepted as true for use in demonstration of another proposition. (2) The argument or theme of a composition prefixed as a title or induction.

LIBERATION. That beyond birth and death that leads to the place of freedom, peace, and happiness. In the Madyamika, that which shows the unreality of everything that we perceive.

MADHYAMIKA. (Sans.) The "Middle" or Middle Way; the philosophical school of Mahayana Buddhism, which emphasizes thinking between absolutism and nihilism. It is derived from the Mahayana (large vehicle) Buddhist philosophy and practice. The school was founded by Nagarjuna (second century A.D.).

MAHAYANA BUDDHISM. (Sans.) "Greater Vehicle." Two major Mahayana schools arose in India: Madhyamika (Middle) and Vijnanavada. With the spread of Mahayana Buddhism beyond India, other schools were formed such as Zen and Tibetan Buddhism.

MAYA. (Sans.) "Illusion" or the illusory perception of the material world.

MIDDLE PATH or WAY. The way to unconditioned, naked awareness. (See MADHYAMIKA.)

MOKSHA. (Sans.) Sometimes spelled *Muksa.* "Liberation."

NAGARJUNA. The dharma-master or philosophic sage from southern India (second century A.D.) who developed one of the most elaborate philosophical systems ever devised within Buddhism, called the Madhyamika. He is also considered the fourteenth patriarch of the Ch'an sect of oriental Buddhism.

NAKED AWARENESS. A state of mind whereby one drops all the baggage of self, subject philosophy, and social conditioning and stands before the mirror to see oneself as a human. Here, the inner dynamics of shortcomings are also understood in the presence of the Absolute.

NIHILISM. Nonexistence. An extreme form of skepticism that denies all existence. Identified with Madhyamika since it is based on the teachings of *sunyata* (emptiness).

NIRVANA. (Sans.) (1) The extinction of desire and individual consciousness, especially in Buddhism, as a beatific state that transcends suffering. (2) A place or state of perfect peace and freedom from pain or suffering.

PARAMARTHA. (Sans.) "Unconditioned life" as the ultimate truth known by Buddhas and bodhisattvas.

PARATRA NIRAPEKSA. (Sans.) "Indifference of place" that is not dependent on something else.

PRAJNA. (Sans.) "Wisdom." Fundamental wisdom that is inherent to every person and can manifest itself only after the veil of ignorance that screens it has been destroyed by means of self-cultivation, as taught by the Buddha, and when the mind is in an internal state of imperturbability, exempt from all external sensation, which is called *samadhi.*

PRAJNAPARAMITA. (Sans.) *Prajna* means "wisdom" and *paramita* means "crossing to the other shore (perfection)"; thus the "Perfection of Wisdom." (1) According to Nagarjuna, the Prajnaparamita consists of the perfect exercise of the wisdom inherent in humanity that destroys all illusions for the purpose of crossing over from this shore of mortality to the other shore of bliss. (2) One of the most important female bodhisattvas in Mahayana Buddhism, representing transcendental wisdom; accordingly, she is regarded as the mystic mother.

PRAJNAPARAMITA SUTRA. (Sans.) The "perfection of Wisdom" corpus central to Mahayana Buddhism, which includes the Diamond Sutra and the Heart Sutra. A profound philosophical-theological teaching that makes it one of the great cornerstones of wisdom literature composed in India, perhaps by Buddha himself and restored in part by Nagarjuna. It is referred to by Indian and Tibetan sages and teachers down through the centuries.

PRATITYA-SAMUTPADA. (Sans.) "Dependent existence" or dependent co-origination.

PUDGALA-NAIRATMYA. (Sans.) Denial of substance of physical matter connected with self or soul existence.

SAMSARA. (Sans.) The realm of birth, death, and rebirth or the continuum that leads to suffering.

SAMVRTI-SATYA. (Sans.) Empirical reality or conventional truth understood by ordinary people.

SANGHA. Precious community of like-minded spiritual friends and practitioners.

SUNYATA. (Sans.) Emptiness or void. In Buddhism, a process whereby physical cognition and human thinking and speech are negated. The experience of "non-self."

SUNYATA-SUNYATA. (Sans.) "Emptiness of emptiness."

SUNYAVADA. (Sans.) Philosophy of emptiness.

SUPERPOSITION. A principle of quantum theory describing the nature and balance of matter and waves at the atomic level, which states that we cannot determine the state of an object.

SUTRA. (Sans.) A philosophical text or grand treatise used for study. In Buddhism, one of the 12 divisions of the Mahayana canon.

SVABHAVA-SUNYA. (Sans.) Devoid of independent reality or not having an independent or intrinsic existence.

TATHAGATA. (Sans.) "Suchness of all Dharmas" according to the Diamond Sutra. Also a title for Buddha or the One who is "Neither Coming nor Going," who takes the way of cause and effect and attains to perfect wisdom.

TATHATA. (Sans.) "Such-ness" or "is-ness," a concept of reality that is timeless and universal.

TETRALEMMA. A group of four logical propositions presented consecutively through which a complex course of negations is offered for mental liberation. The supralogical system of Nagarjuna's classical thinking on overcoming double binds and suffering.

TIME-BINDING. The reality of a subject being fixed or anchored to a fixed time sequence or time consideration, which prevents flexibility and extension of choices or operations by the subject.

TIMELESS. According to Nagarjuna, when the sphere of thought has ceased, the nameable ceases and one acquires the nature that is unrising and unceasing.

TWO-VALUED LOGIC. A logic of two lemmas highly used in Western and Aristotelian formal logic that allows for the reality of the "excluded middle."

VEDAS. Any of four canonical collections (Rig Veda, Sama Veda, Yajur Veda, and Atharva Veda) that comprise the earliest Hindu sacred writings. The Rig Veda is considered the oldest of the four Vedas.

VENN DIAGRAM. A graph that employs circles to represent logical relations between operations on sets and the terms of propositions by the inclusion, exclusion, or intersection of the circles.

VIKALPA. (Sans.) Imagination, conceptualization, or thoughts, also including confusion and fantasy.

Bibliography

A Course in Miracles. Tiburon, CA: Foundation for Inner Peace, 1976.

Almeder, Robert. "A critique of arguments offered against reincarnation." *Journal of Scientific Exploration* 11:4 (1997).

———. *Death and Personal Survival: The Evidence for Life after Death*. Lanham, MD: Rowman and Littlefield, 1992.

Astin, John A., Elaine Harkness, and Edward Ernst. "The efficacy of 'distant healing': A systematic review of randomized trials." *Annals of Internal Medicine* 132:11 (June 2000), pp. 903–910.

Bell, J. S. "On the Einstein, Podolsky, Rosen paradox." *Physics* 1 (1964), pp. 195–200.

Benor, Daniel J. *Spiritual Healing: Scientific Validation of a Healing Revolution [Healing Research, Vol. 1]*. Southfield, MI: Vision Publications, 2001.

Benson, Herbert. *The Relaxation Response*. New York: William Morrow, 1975.

Bohm, David, and B. J. Hiley. *The Undivided Universe: An Ontological Interpretation of Quantum Theory*. New York: Routledge, 1993.

Braud, William. *Distant Mental Influence: Its Contributions to Science, Healing, and Human Interactions*. Charlottesville, VA: Hampton Roads, 2003.

————. "Wellness implications of retroactive intentional influence: Exploring an outrageous hypothesis." *Alternative Therapies in Health and Medicine* 6:1 (2000), pp. 37–48.

Braud, W. G., and M. J. Schlitz. "Consciousness interactions with remote biological systems: Anomalous intentionality effects." *Subtle Energies* 2:1 (1991), pp. 1–46.

Byrd, R. "Positive therapeutic effects of intercessory prayer in a coronary care unit population." *Southern Medical Journal* 81:7 (July 1988), pp. 826–829.

Conze, E. *Buddhism: Its Essence and Development.* New York: Harper & Brothers, 1959.

————. *Buddhist Thought in India.* London: George Allen & Unwin, 1962.

Eccles, John C. *Facing Reality: Philosophical Adventures by a Brain Scientist.* New York: Springer-Verlag, 1970.

Einstein, A., B. Podolsky, and N. Rosen. "Can a quantum mechanical description of physical reality be considered complete?" *Physical Review* 47 (1935), pp. 777–780.

Freedman, S., and J. Clauser. "Experimental test of local hidden variable theories." *Physical Review Letters* 28 (1972), pp. 934-941.

Garfield, Jay L. (trans.). *Fundamental Wisdom of the Middle Way: Nagarjuna's Mulamadhyamakakarika.* New York: Oxford University Press, 1995.

Gödel, K. "Ueber formal unentscheidbare." *Monatshefte fuer Mathematik und Physik* 38 (1931), pp. 173–198.

Harris, W. S., et al. "A randomized, controlled trial of the effects of remote intercessory prayer on outcomes in patients admitted to the coronary care unit." *Archives of Internal Medicine* 159 (October 25, 1999), pp. 2273–2278.

Hurtak, J. J. "Acupuncture and the cycle of birth as viewed in an historic Japanese medical text." *Journal of Alternative and Complementary Medicine* 10:2 (2004).

————. *The Book of Knowledge: The Keys of Enoch®.* Los Gatos, CA: Academy for Future Science, 1973.

————. "The holographic mind as a tool for the evolution of global consciousness," in *Consciousness, Energy, and Future Science.* Los Gatos, CA: Academy for Future Science, 2002.

Huxley, Aldous. *The Doors of Perception.* San Francisco: Panther Press (1977).

Jahn, Robert G., and Brenda J. Dunne. *Margins of Reality: The Role of Consciousness in the Physical World.* San Diego, CA: Harcourt, Brace, Jovanovich, 1987.

Longchenpa. "The Jewel Ship," in *You Are the Eyes of the World.* Ithaca, NY: Snow Lion Publications, 2000.

McFarlane, Thomas. *Sacred Science: Essays on Mathematics, Physics, and Spiritual Philosophy,* 1995, available at: http://www.integral science.org/sacredscience/SS_title.html.

Murti, T. R. V. *The Central Philosophy of Buddhism: A Study of the Madhyamika System.* London: George Allen & Unwin, 1955.

Norbu, Namkhai. *The Mirror: Advice on the Presence of Awareness.* Barrytown, NY: Barrytown, 1996.

Padmasambhava. *Self-Liberation through Seeing with Naked Awareness,* tr. John Myrdhin Reynolds. Ithaca, NY: Snow Lion Publications, 2000.

Pert, Candace. *Molecules of Emotion: The Science behind Mind-Body Medicine.* New York: Scribner, 1999.

Playfair, Guy Lyon. *Twin Telepathy: The Psychic Connection.* London: Vega, 2002.

Prabhavananda, Swami, and Christopher Isherwood (trans.). *How to Know God.* Hollywood, CA: Vedanta Press, 1983.

————. *Shankara's Crest-jewel of Discrimination.* Hollywood, CA: Vedanta Press, 1978.

Puthoff, H. E., and R. Targ. "A perceptual channel for information transfer over kilometer distances: Historical perspective and recent research." *Proceedings of the IEEE* 64:3 (1976).

Puthoff, H. E., R. Targ, and E. C. May. "Experimental psi research: Implications for physics," in R. G. Jahn, *The Role of Consciousness in the Physical World, AAAS Selected Symposium 57*. Boulder, CO: Westview Press, 1981.

Radin, Dean I. *The Conscious Universe: The Scientific Truth of Psychic Phenomena*. New York: HarperEdge, 1997.

Rauscher, E. A., and R. Targ. "The speed of thought: Investigation of a complex space-time metric to describe psychic phenomena." *Journal of Scientific Exploration* 15:3 (Fall 2001), pp. 331–354.

Rhine, L. "Frequency and types of experience in spontaneous precognition." *Journal of Parapsychology* 6 (1954), pp. 93–123.

Robinson, Richard H. *Early Madhyamika in India and China*. Madison: University of Wisconsin Press, 1967.

———. *Madhyamika Studies in Fifth-Century China*. London thesis, 1959.

Rubik, B., and E. Rauscher. "Effects on motility behavior and growth rate of *Salmonella typhimurium* in the presence of a psychic subject," in W. G. Roll (ed.), *Research in Parapsychology*. Metuchen, NJ: Scarecrow Press, 1979, pp. 140–142.

Schlitz, M., and W. Braud. "Distant intentionality and healing: Assessing the evidence," *Alternative Therapies in Health and Medicine* 3:6 (November 1997).

Schrödinger, Erwin. *What Is Life? The Physical Aspect of the Living Cell*. Cambridge, England: Cambridge University Press, 1944.

Sherman, Harold. *Your Power to Heal*. New York: Harper & Row, 1972.

Sicher, F., E. Targ, D. Moore, and H. Smith. "A randomized double-blind study of the effect of distant healing in a population with advanced AIDS." *Western Journal of Medicine* 169 (December 1998), pp. 356–363.

Stapp, Henry, in Robert Nadeau and Menas Kafatos. *The Non-local Universe: The New Physics and Matters of the Mind*. New York: Oxford University Press, 1999.

Stcherbatsky, Th. *The Conception of Buddhist Nirvana.* The Hague: Mouton, 1965, citing the *Madhyamika-Sastra* XVIII:9.

Stevenson, Ian. *Children Who Remember Previous Lives.* Charlottesville, VA: University Press of Virginia, 1987.

———. *Twenty Cases Suggestive of Reincarnation.* New York: American Society for Psychical Research, 1966.

———. *Where Reincarnation and Biology Intersect.* Westport, CT: Praeger, 1997.

Suzuki, T. *On Indian Mahayana Buddhism.* New York: Harper & Row, 1968.

Sylvia, Claire. *A Change of Heart.* New York: Little Brown, 1997.

Targ, Elisabeth. "Evaluating distant healing: A research review." *Alternative Therapies in Health and Medicine* 3:6 (November 1977).

Targ, Russell, and Jane Katra. *Miracles of Mind: Exploring Nonlocal Consciousness and Spiritual Healing.* Novato, CA: New World Library, 1998.

Targ, Russell, and Harold Puthoff. "Information transfer under conditions of sensory shielding." *Nature* 251 (1974), pp. 602–607.

Tittel, W., J. Brendel, H. Zbinden, and N. Gisin. "Violation of Bell inequalities by photons more than 10 km apart." *Physical Review Letters* 81:17 (1998), pp. 3563–3566.

Traitz, James. *Don't Stop Your Mind.* Cleveland, OH: Arete Press, 2003.

Vassy, Zoltán. "Method for measuring the probability of 1 bit extrasensory information transfer between living organisms." *Journal of Parapsychology* 42 (1978), pp. 158–160.

Wallace, B. Alan. *Choosing Reality: A Contemplative View of Physics and the Mind.* Boston: New Science Library, 1989.

Watts, Alan. *The Way of Zen.* New York: Pantheon, 1957.

Winters, Jonah. *Thinking in Buddhism: Nagarjuna's Middle Way,* dissertation for Reed College in Portland, Oregon, 1994, available at: http://bahai_library.com/personal/jw/other.pubs/.

Suggested Bibliography for Additional Reading

A Course in Miracles: Workbook for Students. Huntington Station, NY: Foundation for Inner Peace, 1975.

Curtis, B., and J. J. Hurtak. "Consciousness and quantum information processing: Uncovering the foundation for a medicine of light," *Journal of Alternative and Complementary Medicine 10* (2004), pp. 27–39.

Dossey, Larry. *Healing Words: The Power of Prayer and the Practice of Medicine.* San Francisco, CA: HarperSanFrancisco, 1993, pp. 127–132.

Dunne, B., R. Nelson, and R. Jahn. "Operator related anomalies in a random mechanical cascade." *Journal of Scientific Exploration* 2:2 (1978), pp. 155–179.

Gangaji. *Freedom and Resolve: The Living Edge of Surrender.* Novato, CA: Gangaji Foundation, 1999.

Hameroff, S. R. "Quantum coherence in microtubules: A neural basis for emergent consciousness?" *Journal of Consciousness Studies* 1 (1994), pp. 91–118.

Harman, W. W., and C. DeQuincey. *The Scientific Exploration of Consciousness: Toward an Adequate Epistemology.* Sausalito, CA: Institute of Noetic Sciences, 1994.

Harpur, Tom. *The Uncommon Touch: An Investigation of Spiritual Healing.* Toronto: McClelland & Steward, 1994.

Hearne, K. "An ostensible precognition using a 'dream machine.'" *Journal of the Society for Psychological Research* 53:799 (1985), pp. 38–40.

Honorton, C. "Psi and internal attention states." *Handbook of Parapsychology.* New York: Van Nostrand Reinhold, 1977.

Hurtak, J. J. *Consciousness, Energy, and Future Science.* Los Gatos, CA: Academy for Future Science, 2002.

———. "Distant intentionality on biological systems: Healing at a distance," *Proceedings from Quantum Mind Conference,* Tucson, AZ: University of Arizona, April 2003.

————. "New thinkers, God, and holism in the twenty-first century," *Journal of Future History* 6 (2004), pp. 6–11.

Idel, Moshe. *Kabbalah: New Perspectives.* New Haven, CT: Yale University Press, 1988, pp. xiii–xv.

Jahn, Robert. "The persistent paradox of psychic phenomena: An engineering perspective." *IEEE,* 70:3 (1982), pp. 64–104.

————. *The Role of Consciousness in the Physical World.* Boulder, CO: Westview Press, 1981.

Jahn, R., B. Dunne, and E. Jahn. "Analytical judging procedure for remote perception experiments," *Journal of Parapsychology* 3 (1980), pp. 207–231.

Jampolsky, Gerald. *Love Is Letting Go of Fear.* Berkeley, CA: Celestial Arts, 1979.

Kushner, Lawrence. *The River of Light.* Woodstock, VT: Jewish Lights, 1981.

Longchenpa. *Kindly Bent to Ease Us,* tr. Herbert V. Guenther. Emeryville, CA: Dharma, 1975.

————. *The Precious Treasury of the Basic Space of Phenomena.* Junction City, CA: Padma Pub., 2001.

————. *The Precious Treasury of the Way of Abiding and the Exposition of the Quintessential Meaning of the Three Categories.* Junction City, CA: Padma Pub., 1998.

May, E., and L. Vilenskaya. "Some aspects of parapsychological research in the former Soviet Union." *Subtle Energies* 3 (1994), pp. 1–24.

Monroe, Robert. *Journeys Out of the Body.* New York: Broadway Books, 1973.

Myers, F. W. H. *Human Personality and Its Survival of Bodily Death.* Charlottesville, VA: Hampton Roads, 2001.

Pribram, Karl. *The Brain II Millennium.* Los Angeles: J. Tarcher, 1981, pp. 91–104.

Radin, D., F. Machado, and W. Zangari. *Proceedings of Presented Papers: The 41st Annual Convention of the Parapsychological Association.*

Halifax, Nova Scotia, Canada: Parapsychological Investigations, 1998: 143–161.

Radin, D., and R. Nelson. "Evidence for consciousness-related anomalies in random physical systems." *Foundations of Physics* 19 (1989), pp. 1499–1514.

Schrödinger, Erwin. *My View of the World.* Woodbridge, CT: Ox Bow Press, 1983.

Sinclair, Upton. *Mental Radio.* Charlottesville, VA: Hampton Roads, 2001.

Stapp, Henry P. *Mind, Matter, and Quantum Mechanics.* Berlin, Germany: Springer-Verlag, 1993.

Targ, E., R. Targ, and O. Lichtarg. "Realtime clairvoyance: Study of remote viewing without feedback." *Journal of the American Society for Psychical Research* 79 (October 1985), pp. 494–500.

Targ, Russell. *Limitless Mind: A Guide to Remote Viewing and Transformation of Consciousness.* Novato, CA: New World Library, 2004.

Targ, Russell, and Keith Harary. *The Mind Race: Understanding and Using Psychic Abilities.* New York: Villard Books, 1984.

Targ, R., and J. Katra. "Remote viewing in a group setting." *Journal of Scientific Exploration* 14:1 (2000), pp. 107–114.

Targ, R., and H. Puthoff. "Direct perception of remote geographic locations." *Mind at Large: IEEE Symposia on the Nature of Extrasensory Perception.* Charlottesville, VA: Hampton Roads, 2002.

———. "Information transmission under conditions of sensory shielding." *Nature* 251 (1974), pp. 602–607.

———. *Mind-Reach: Scientists Look at Psychic Abilities.* New York: Delacorte, 1977, and Charlottesville, VA: Hampton Roads, 2005.

Weinberg, Steven. "The future of science and the universe." *New York Review of Books* (November 15, 2001).

Wilber, Ken. *One Taste: Daily Reflections on Integral Spirituality.* Boston: Shambhala, 1999.

Index

(page numbers in italics refer to pictures)

About the Authors

Russell Targ is a physicist and author, a pioneer in the development of the laser and laser applications, and cofounder of the Stanford Research Institute's investigation into psychic abilities in the 1970s and 1980s. His work in this new area, called remote viewing, was published in *Nature, Proceedings of the Institute of Electrical and Electronics Engineers (IEEE)*, and *Proceedings of the American Association for the Advancement of Science.*

Targ has a bachelor's degree in physics from Queens College and did graduate work in physics at Columbia University. He received two National Aeronautics and Space Administration awards for inventions and contributions to lasers and laser communications; and he accepted invitations in 1983 and 1984 to present remote viewing demonstrations and to address the USSR Academy of Sciences on this research.

He is coauthor of five books dealing with the scientific investigation of psychic abilities, including *Mind-Reach: Scientists Look at Psychic Abilities* (republished in 2005) and *Limitless Mind: A Guide to Remote Viewing and Transformation of Consciousness.*

As a senior staff scientist at Lockheed Martin Missiles & Space Company, Targ developed airborne laser systems for the detection of wind shear. He retired in 1997 and now pursues ESP research in Palo Alto, California. He is also publishing special editions of classic books in psychical research. His website is www.espresearch.com.

J. J. Hurtak, Ph.D., is a social scientist, philosopher, and futurist. He holds graduate degrees from the University of California (Ph.D.) and the University of Minnesota (Ph.D.). In oriental studies, he worked with Vietnamese Buddhist scholar Dr. Thich Tien-An and helped to microfilm the Tibetan canon in Nepal and India.

Hurtak, with his wife Desiree, has published a complete translation and commentary on the *Pistis Sophia* texts of early Gnostic Christianity. He is president of the Academy for Future Science (www.futurescience.org), an international nonprofit organization that is involved with the dialogue regarding the issues of science and religion. He has also done archaeological research in Mexico and Egypt, where he was instrumental in finding the Osiris tomb (1997).

In his capacity as an international consultant, Hurtak has been featured in numerous film documentaries and has been on television radio programs throughout the world, including *Evening Magazine, 60 Minutes* (International), *Good Morning Australia, Good Morning South Africa,* the international ECO-satellite program *2020,* BBC Radio, and Coast to Coast AM. He has won eight gold medal awards from international film festivals for his graphic films and animation on consciousness exploration: *Merkabah, Initiation,* and his latest, *The Light Body.* He was also a technical consultant for Sidney Sheldon's bestseller *The Doomsday Conspiracy.*

Hampton Roads Publishing Company

. . . for the evolving human spirit

HAMPTON ROADS PUBLISHING COMPANY publishes books on a variety of subjects, including metaphysics, spirituality, health, visionary fiction, and other related topics.

For a copy of our latest trade catalog, call toll-free, 800-766-8009, or send your name and address to:

HAMPTON ROADS PUBLISHING COMPANY, INC.
1125 STONEY RIDGE ROAD • CHARLOTTESVILLE, VA 22902
e-mail: hrpc@hrpub.com • www.hrpub.com